Isabelle Jan's *On Children's Literature* will be of great interest both to parents with children who enjoy reading and to all adults who remember the books they read as children and perhaps still enjoy.

The author sets out to consider children's literature as a distinct *genre*: its history, the way it has developed in response to changing social conditions, the extent to which adult writers have imposed their own tastes and concerns on their child readers, and what it is that makes particular books popular with children. She avoids a long chronological survey; having considered the sources of children's literature in folktale and ballad and the first written children's literature in the eighteenth century, she proceeds to explore the subject thematically and in relation to its notable authors. She examines in detail the work of Hans Andersen, Lear and Carroll, and the themes of the hero, the family, animals, and adventure.

Isabelle Jan's knowledge is extraordinarily wide: her discussion takes into account the work of authors of sixteen countries. But the real value of the book lies elsewhere: in her brilliant insights into specific authors and books. The author most effectively relates to her literary judgements a clear knowledge of both psychology and sociology. She is equally interesting talking about the imagination of P. L. Travers, the author of *Mary Poppins*, or children's deeply-rooted fascination and nostalgia for the apparent security of the animal world, or the emergence of the Dickensian child-hero in response to the industrial revolution.

This is an extremely intelligent book written with wit and lightness of touch. It is valuable both for some highly original litera— criticism and f⟨ ⟩ ⟨ ⟩ affords ⟨ ⟩ imagination of

D0966148

Isabelle Jan

On children's literature

Translated from the French

Edited and with a preface by Catherine Storr

Allen Lane

First published in 1969
by Les Éditions ouvrières, Paris
Copyright © Les Éditions ouvrières, 1969

This translation first published in Great Britain in 1973
Allen Lane
A Division of Penguin Books Ltd
21 John Street, London WCIN 2BT
Translation copyright © Allen Lane, 1973

ISBN 0 7139 0213 2

Printed in Great Britain by
Ebenezer Baylis and Son Ltd,
The Trinity Press, Worcester, and London

Set in Monotype Garamond

Contents

Preface

by Catherine Storr

The question with which Professor Isabelle Jan prefaces her essay on the subject of children's literature is, whether or not such a body or work exists. If it does, what are its hall-marks? How do we recognize it? Is there really such a category at all, or are there only books intended for young readers, and others which are what the young do in fact read? Is there no such thing as 'children's literature' at all?

Perhaps it is an academic rather than a practical question, and I hope that the reader who is more interested in the facts than in the theory won't be misled into believing that it is of prime importance, either to him or to Mlle Jan. Because, whether or not the category exists, in library catalogues, in the minds of students of literature, or in the indices of learned volumes, we all know that there is a category of books which children enjoy; and as Mlle Jan says in her last chapter, it is the child's enjoyment of a book which gives it its strongest claim to be considered as 'children's literature'. What Mlle Jan is really doing in this short and perceptive study is not to tell us that there is or isn't a body of work which can be definitively included under this ambiguous heading, but to consider the books them-selves which, whether written for children or not, children want to read.

For the last fifteen years in this country there has been no shortage of people thinking and writing seriously about books for children. In recent years there have been numerous periodicals devoted to the review of recently published children's books, to articles on the relevance of these books to education, to advice to parents and teachers on the reading matter of their young charges. Weekly periodicals give up what sometimes amounts to a surprising amount of space to the bi-annual or even quarterly review of the some 2,000 books published in Britain each year for children. There have also been more or less comprehensive histories of Juvenilia – as second-hand book catalogues call it – such as Gillian Avery's *Nineteenth Century Children* and John Rowe Townsend's *Written for Children*. What we haven't yet had in this country, however, is a study of the genre, a close, reasoned and perceptive inquiry into the essence of the thing itself; and this is what Mlle Jan now offers us.

She seems uniquely qualified for the task; for she has not only the objectivity and critical powers of the intellectual, but also the intuitive perception of the poet. She is widely read – as one might expect – in her own language, and has apparently also read books for children from England, America, Sweden, Italy, Brazil, Hungary, Russia, and, doubtless, other countries too. More than this, she has the capacity to understand the peculiarly English idiom to so great an extent that I must suppose, though obviously I can't judge at first hand, that she instinctively understands that of other countries foreign to her. We, in England, often suppose with, perhaps, insular pride that no one who hasn't been brought up with a background of English nursery rhymes, English jokes, English poetry and English nursery lore, can possibly appreciate Lewis Carroll's Alice; how is it then, that Mlle Jan writes the most acute and the most intuitive account of the Alice books that I have ever read? Not a Freudian interpretation, but a survey of what the books are about in ordinary human terms. She sees that Alice's predicament is not that she cannot wake up from a

dream, but that she cannot successfully fit herself into surroundings for which she, in virtue of her reality – and her
common sense – is never the right size . . . Alice standing
on a threshold which cannot be crossed. In the same terms
Mlle Jan recognizes that Mme de Ségur's Sophie suffers
always from the fact that she constantly destroys – toys,
animals, friendships, her own appearance – and is then
punished for her involuntary destructiveness.

When she writes about Hans Christian Andersen, Mlle
Jan is equally illuminating. He, she believes, uniquely com-
bines these unconscious obsessions retained from childhood,
which inform a writer's choice of images, and also the
capacity – what Keats called 'negative capability' – to allow
those symbols to speak for themselves. She draws a contrast
between writers, like Andersen, who are led into the story
by the characters, and those like Dumas and Jules Verne,
who write 'adventure stories', in which the plot is imposed
on the characters and takes pride of place; it is the difference
between the inward-looking writer who dwells on situations
which mirror his own preoccupations, and the outward-
looking writer to whom action is more important. Whether
she is considering the poets, or the adventure writers, the
moralists, or writers of stories about animals, or the classic
fairy stories whose authors are not single individuals but
peoples, Mlle Jan speaks always with the voice of common
sense, learning and perceptive appreciation. Her conclusions
may perhaps have surprised herself. She finds that the real
literature for children is written by those who can conduct
a dialogue between themselves as adults and the children
they once were. Whether these writers are poets, writing
about their own problems, or the seekers after treasure in
the form of a story, in each case the writing must be in a
form which children can accept; that is, it must be understood from the child's position, written for the child within
the author, not for the child whom the author observes. She

1*

believes that boredom, a surfeit of second-hand themes, unimaginatively played on, is the chief danger to be feared in 'children's literature'; she pleads, in her final chapter, for the possibility of the fresh, the poetic approach, which alone can 'surprise by joy'.

1. *Introduction*

Is there such a thing as a literature for children? In countries where literacy and primary education have become the norm, a large proportion of books published are, indeed, for children; apart from textbooks and educational works a very wide choice of picture- and story-books reach the market. But because publishers print books for children, and because children read certain books, we cannot instantly assume that a specific 'children's literature' exists. When we examine the nature and purpose of such works we shall inevitably judge them not only according to the extent of their readership but also from an aesthetic, educational and even ideological point of view. At once our initial question becomes more complex: do these purely entertaining books for children have the same right as more mature works of literary expression to be seen as works of creative imagination? Do they play a significant part in a child's intellectual and perceptual development? Do the authors, even if unintentionally, use them to express the ideals of the society that produces them? To what extent do concerned adults such as parents and teachers allow their own tastes and preconceptions to influence how the child will react to a particular book?

Until quite recently comprehensive literary histories have not included writers for children as such. In the very rare instances where an author is classified as a children's writer, he is invariably related to one trend or another of imaginative expression, and literary historians appear to ignore the basic distinction of his being primarily a writer for children, as though this were a detail of no real significance. Research in this field has, until now, been carried out mainly by educationalists and sociologists whose approach is determined by their professional concerns and who have therefore concentrated their attention on the role of books in the lives of contemporary children.

Apart from the specialist attitude it is possible to single out at least four particular categories of books which the non-specialist adult generally regards as constituting children's literature. The first is picture books and comic strips; the second is fairy tales and folklore; the third consists of fragments of masterpieces originally written for adults, which, when they've been suitably abridged and bowdlerized, are considered suitable for children. The fourth main category is the 'children's classics', books written especially for children but which often represent only part of the author's total output, like Carroll's Alice books, *Pinocchio*, Ruskin's *King of the Golden River*, Hardy's *Our Exploits at West Foley*, Saint Exupéry's *Little Prince*. But of these four categories only the last comes within the scope of this inquiry: picture books and comic strips cannot really be considered as literature because the interest is centred on the illustrations and not on the text – though Beatrix Potter's witty and economical prose could almost stand by itself; fairy stories and folklore belonged originally as much to adults as to children; and excerpts from books intended for adult reading, like parts of Dickens's novels, or whole works which have insensibly slipped from the adult to the children's shelves, like *Robinson Crusoe* and *Gulliver*, should not rightly be classified as literature for children. And those books which can be so categorized, 'the classics', meant for children and tailored to their needs, have until quite recently tended to be exceptional works by otherwise 'serious' writers, rather than the natural output of a recognized literary genre.

This state of affairs, however, no longer holds. Today we have a real literature for children which is continuously evolving and changing, partly in response to its own readership, partly from its own dynamism. It is a literature with distinct antecedents, which has developed its own characteristic features, its particular identity, both from its past and its correspondence to changing social conditions.

The state of children's literature varies of course from country to country. Where there has been a high social and economic standard for some time, so that a large proportion of the children are literate and have enough time for an unremunerative occupation like reading, one would expect to find it flourishing, and this is borne out in most European countries, in North America, in Latin America and Japan. Various differences between these countries will influence the sort of children's literature they produce: in some, ideological and educational tenets hinder the growth of any really original works: Catholic and Protestant countries produce different books for children;[1] there are differences also between countries like Britain and Scandinavia, for instance, where schools are not only institutions of learning but also of education and recreation, and countries like France, where children go to school only to acquire knowledge; and the privileged position of children's literature in Britain and the U.S.A. is explained partly by the effective operation of the public library systems.

Another general point which is worth making at this stage is that the development of the children's literature in any particular country is closely dependent on the strength of its

1. This point of view has been thoroughly examined by Paul Hazard in *Les livres, les enfants, les hommes*, Flammarion, Paris, 1932, a book which is still the best comprehensive essay on the subject to date.

own literary tradition. One example of this is the way in which the oral tradition has survived in different countries. A number of the best writers in Russia, for instance, from Pushkin via Gogol to Tolstoy, took their inspiration from national folklore. The illiterate story-teller, Arina Rodionova, Pushkin's old nurse, or the peasants Alexei Tolstoy discovered and introduced to a wide and cultured audience, became as much respected as their writer colleagues, for in Russia there is no basic distinction, no absolute frontier, between written and oral literatures and even today young Soviet poets recite their poems in front of an audience before publishing them. This is even more striking in the case of children's literature, of which a substantial portion, including the classic *Little Hunchback Horse* by Erchov[2] and the works of the contemporary poet Ania Barto, continue, as a result of oral tradition, to be written in verse.

In America a group led by the story-teller Sara Cone Bryant is trying to promote a revival of oral tradition by organizing a 'story hour' in some schools and children's libraries, thus putting the pleasures of listening on an equal footing with those of reading; but it is not a spontaneous activity as it is in Russia, and its bias is mainly educational. Such an experiment, however, does indicate a tendency to stress the importance of an essential ingredient of poetry – rhythm.

But in France, there is scarcely any poetry for children. It seems that a literature with a lively oral tradition, where poetry is recited, declaimed and sung, where, as in Walt Whitman's work, the ear is delighted by cascades of words, will be more readily accessible to children than a literature like the French where the clarity and elegance of the writing has absolute priority. The French child is invariably made to read La Fontaine, a poet who is not only so difficult to

2. For biographical and bibliographical notes on writers and works quoted see the list at the end of the book.

read out loud that his poems are a virtuoso exercise for students at the Conservatoire, but is also a poet who must be *read* because the typography and layout are intimately related to the verse.

To reach a proper definition of the nature of children's literature we must see it as a whole and examine it comparatively. The approach must be one of synthesis rather than analysis and no arbitrary pattern should be imposed. A geographical division, therefore, into French, British, or German literature will not suffice because this would imply a fragmentation and would emphasize local colour too strongly. A chronological survey would preclude any attempt at definition. Examples and references will necessarily be restricted and arbitrarily chosen, because only by assuming full responsibility for such high-handedness, by omitting – sometimes unfairly – certain works, or over-emphasizing others, can an inquiry take shape and progress. The problem is to discover the characteristic features of the genre and what constitutes its unvarying core, respecting the natural time sequence, but avoiding historical bias.

Collector's pieces (such as those Japanese scrolls with pictures of anthropomorphic animals so charming that they might be the ancestors of Mr Toad or Peter Rabbit)[3] or the few medieval tales about child-heroes, are outside the scope of this survey, but we do know, apart from these, which were the first books written for children, and the most interesting is unquestionably *Pictus Orbis* (1657) by the humanist, Jan Amos Comenius, a pioneer of Czech literature. This is an ABC cum treatise of ethics and natural history written in the form of a dialogue between 'the boy' and 'the master' but, most important, it was the first picture book for children. Comenius's basic – and remarkably modern – idea

3. Cf. Toba Sojo, *The Illustrated Scroll*, dating from the twelfth century, preserved at the Temple of Kozanji, in Kyoto, published by G. P. Putman's Sons & Co., New York, 1954.

was that any object named to a child should simultaneously be shown to him and so the book is decorated with numerous illustrations, beautifully executed in Nuremberg.

Two other seventeenth-century writers who contributed to children's literature were John Bunyan with *Pilgrim's Progress* (1676) and Fénelon with his *Fables*, *Dialogues des morts*, and *Télémaque* (1699), three books written expressly for the young Duke of Burgundy. Both these authors use their plots as a vehicle for moral and religious instruction and the symbolism becomes a rather heavy allegory. They were isolated, purely didactic works not intended for a mass readership but for a privileged minority, in Fénelon's case for one particular child. As long as we are dealing with exceptions, even exemplary ones, we cannot rightly refer to a literature, because the term presupposes a continuing publication. But seventeenth- and eighteenth-century child readers – along with the mass of the people – did have reading matter in the form of pamphlets hawked by pedlars: the *Bibliothèque bleue* in France and chapbooks in Britain. In these they found a medley of tales, legends, folklore, moral precepts and abridged classics. In France, after 1840, Pellerin set up the Epinal press, and illustrations became an integral part of this literature.

But it was in England that the idea of publications for children first took root. In 1745, near St Paul's Cathedral in the City, a certain John Newbery opened a little stall at the sign of *The Bible and Sun*. This was the first bookshop to cater exclusively for children and for over twenty years Newbery published cheap little books, skilfully illustrated, called the *Little Pretty Pocket Books* which sold to an ever-increasing public. When one thinks of the cultural status of neighbouring countries at the time, such a venture stands out as a landmark – almost as an anachronism. Indeed, growing up in a world which was only just beginning to notice the fact that childhood existed, English children were exceptionally lucky. Newbery, who was a fellow-citizen and almost a contemporary of Locke, may be seen as the founder of children's literature. He was, nevertheless, a man of his time and his work bore its imprint; if the presentation of his books was a breakthrough, their content was still subject to contemporary social prejudices and psychological limitations. These demanded practical knowledge and a rigid, unimaginative morality, which is exactly what he provided. Yet his earlier publications did make some concessions to fantasy; he was one of the first to realize that children want to be told stories and that the best stories are still the traditional tales of days gone by; he may have guessed that children require the kind of stories they make up for themselves, and that they enjoy reading the counting rhymes and jingles that feature so largely in their games. Thus the first collection of *Nursery Rhymes* was published. Newbery's publications then, are more than collectors' pieces; they open out new vistas on the beginnings of children's literature and enable us to formulate a new question: Who were the children who read the *Little Pretty Pocket Books*?

2. *Didactic Influences*

Before a special children's literature can develop, childhood must be recognized as a separate state of being. In medieval Europe, as in the classical world, there were children – or at least little men and women who were hardly more childish than their elders and already conditioned by the obligations of their class – but was there such a concept as childhood? Not at any rate as we now think of it, so that when Rousseau exclaimed, 'childhood is unknown'[1] it was the beginning of a new era – a new world was discovered. In a century of revolutions this was the most significant, as decisive and total as that of Copernicus.

Note that Rousseau did not say 'children' but 'childhood': everybody knew about children – they were the little peasants, serfs, lords and ladies – only childhood was an unknown concept: 'Even the wisest try to discover the man in the child without asking themselves what was there before manhood'.[2] Before manhood there was the unfathomable and enthralling world of childhood. He who has once returned to that world can no longer ignore it: 'Love childhood, its games, its delights, its instinctive sweetness'. Yes, the idea of childhood, like that of happiness, was new to Europe. Its discovery was not the result of an intellectual process; no one held an inquiry into the conditions of

1. J.-J. Rousseau, *Émile, ou l'Éducation*, preface (1762).
2. ibid.

children's lives or exposed a state of affairs with paradoxes
and abuses which he proposed to amend. It was discovered
in moments of individual insight and could not be described
in clear factual terms but was at first more a feeling of
instinctive sympathy. Childhood was to be found in one's
own consciousness through one's own memories. And of all
the eighteenth-century philosophers, Jean-Jacques Rousseau
who, in the words of Bernard Groethuysen, saw himself as
'a stranger among men', felt himself to be made of a different clay, was to be the first to experience, understand and
try to express the estrangement felt by those other social
misfits, children.

Rousseau had always been searching for a nature as
unpolished but as true as an uncut diamond and this he
found in childhood. He did not see the state as an obscure
promise not yet fulfilled; its weaknesses and paradoxes did
not appear to be shortcomings that an enlightened education would rectify; on the contrary, they were positive
qualities to be encouraged as safeguards against society's on-
slaughts and the distortions of an overwrought imagination.
Not only must we be aware of the contamination of society
– a warning often absurdly overemphasized – but also of
unduly indulging the imagination.

The books Rousseau read as a child had helped to create
an imaginary world that cut him off from reality and was
'peopled with beings after his own heart'. In this world he
dwelt all his life and experienced greater joy in it than any
man had ever experienced before, but it made him into 'the
most unhappy of men'. Thus, his main preoccupation in
educating Émile was to preserve him from a similar fate.
The book is a desperate attempt to regain contact with
reality, and Émile's education consists in exercising his
mind and his senses to perceive the world in its entirety as
it truly is. His senses and his emotions were to respond
only to actual events, to things that really happen. Men

should lead real, not imaginary lives and to this end they must avoid everything that works directly on the imagination and be encouraged to react to what is real and concrete.

This obsession with reality at the expense of fantasy advocated in *Émile* gradually came to dominate Rousseau's whole existence. His whole didactic philosophy was based on the idea of preserving man's initial integrity of body and soul by what he called 'negative education'. This consisted first of all in prolonging childhood: 'Let childhood ripen in children . . . ' and in favouring its natural tendencies. If a child evinces a lively, adaptable intelligence this should not be seen as the sign of a mature mind capable of logical deductions. In other words, a child should not be introduced to emotions, knowledge or thoughts until he is ready to experience, assimilate and understand them naturally and entirely. His aptitude both for learning and for feeling should not at any time be overtaxed. The theory of a universal level of knowledge should be replaced by a new standard of what it is useful for the individual to know at any given time:

No, if nature has endowed children with a supple brain apt to receive all kinds of impressions, it is not so that it can be encumbered with the names and dates of kings or with heraldic, astronomical and geographical terms – lists of words which are devoid of significance at that age and of practical utility at any age whatsoever – and which render their existence miserable and sterile. A child's memory is not of such a kind that it is reduced to idleness if he does not pore over books; everything he sees and hears leaves its impression on his mind so that he remembers it.3

Particularly where moral education is concerned, a total void is better than artificiality, and a child who behaves as amorally as a young animal is preferable to one who is mechanically submissive to pre-established principles. For a

3. *Émile*, Book II.

child's unawakened conscience cannot grasp moral precepts which do not correspond to any personal experience ... Negative education, finally, will avoid forming rigid thought patterns which only make a child's mind sterile.

Rousseau's attitude to literature may be deduced from this brief summary of the more revolutionary aspects of his educational philosophy. Learning must, obviously, never take its impetus from books (his reaction to the plethora of encyclopedias and over-simplified handbooks which sub-merges today's children does not bear thinking about!). But his policy is just as uncompromising towards imaginative works which fix a child's emotional attitude before he has had time to develop naturally. Indeed, in the emotional as well as in the intellectual sphere Émile must be spared every form of mediation; he must never have his introduction to emotions filtered through an adult sensibility.

Rousseau's message was understood and applied in one of two ways: either it was swallowed whole and a negative education – which is a contradiction in terms – was in fact adopted; or certain (not necessarily the best) aspects of his method were retained and the 'book of nature' was propped open for the child's benefit so that his mind could be edified all the time and at every opportunity.

The latter attitude was adopted by the French, German and English governesses of the generation that followed Rousseau. It was not until the beginning of the twentieth century that the spirit of his didactic philosophy was understood and his method discarded.

Rousseau definitely stated: no books for children. But the eighteenth-century governesses and educators nearly all wrote children's books. In France, Madame Leprince de Beaumont published in 1757 *Le Magasin des enfants*, Madame de Genlis, *Théâtre à l'usage des jeunes personnes* (1779) followed by *Adèle et Théodore ou lettres sur l'éducation* (1782) and, most important, *Veillées du château* (1784) while in 1783 Berquin

contributed *L'Ami des enfants*. In England Laetitia Barbauld,
Sarah Trimmer, Sarah Fielding and Thomas Day were no
less formidable and prolific writers than Madame de Genlis,
and in Germany, Christian-Felix Weiss was writing edifying
rhymes for children and publishing a magazine called
Kinderfreund. Thus the second half of the eighteenth century
saw a steady flow of stilted literature, totally unreadable
today, that penetrated aristocratic and middle-class homes
alike and, unaffected by the revolutionary intermission,
lived on happily to the beginning of the nineteenth. Paul
Hazard[4] has written a brilliant analysis of this type of
literature which, 'created for (children) seems to ignore what
they want and what they like, opposes some of their most
positive tastes and is totally unsuited for them; so much so
that it strikes us today as a vast rubbish heap'.

All these books had two objectives: to inform and to
edify. 'Adèle and Théodore, like all children, are fond of
playing at Mother and Father. Under my supervision this
game has become a true lesson in moral standards', Madame
de Genlis declares. These books have nothing that could
appeal to a child, no plot and a purely social – therefore
dated and absurd – moral outlook and are equally devoid of
style. They are totally lacking in charm and lightness of
touch, and not only have the writers failed to create a distinctive form, they have not even had the sense to adapt a
traditional form to assist them on their pedestrian way, such
as the short story or the inventions of the *Commedia dell'
Arte*, where they might have found inspiration from authors
like Voltaire or Marivaux. They remain, on the contrary,
petrified in the worst conventions of such drawing-room
literature as letters, dialogues and uninspired, static comedy
situations.

The characters – each encapsulated in a role – are called
names like Miss Good, Lady Sensible, Lady Witty, Miss

4. op cit.

Mary Peace, Schoolmaster Philotechnos or Doctor Chronickel. Berquin (the prototype of such writers) goes to ridiculous extremes of artificiality and explicitness; each of his playlets is written with the definite aim of leaving the child reader either the wiser in one specific field, or cured of one particular vice, or informed of the fate reserved for those who commit some error. The dialogue form – question and answer – establishes a spurious relationship between author and reader, besides compelling the hero to be always on scene acting his part of disobedient, selfish, wilful or otherwise unpleasant child. Rousseau's comment on such literature can be found in a letter to Madame d'Épinay who was wont to try her hand at it:

Madame, I have read with the utmost attention your letters to your son; they are beautiful and excellent but they can be of no use to him ... I believe that the idea of writing to him is a happy one and might greatly assist the development of his heart and his mind, but on two conditions: That he may be permitted to understand and to respond ... Make up tales, make up fables, from which he can draw his own moral conclusions and which he can turn to his own personal use. Beware of generalizations; when facts are replaced by maxims they become diffuse and unconvincing; you should proceed from things he may have observed himself, whether in good or in ill. When his ideas have begun to evolve and you have shown him how to think and to judge for himself you can adjust the tone of your letters to his progress and aptitude. But if you tell your son that you are setting out to mould his heart and his mind, that while entertaining him you will be teaching him the truth and his duty, he will be wary of everything that you say; he will expect nothing but edification from you and come to regard everything, even his top, with suspicion.

Rousseau laid bare a child's innermost thoughts ... But it was a flash of genius that enlightened neither his contemporaries nor his successors. For a century children continued to be misunderstood, deprived of attention and compassion. They had, indeed, been given a voice in didactic literature, but it was an unfamiliar voice which they could not recognize as their own. Instead of the natural beings Rousseau had dreamt of, children were turned into the social puppets he loathed. There was not a single educator gifted enough to invent literature for children, or a poet who could make them speak.

We should not, however, infer that didactic literature was foredoomed as such, though many years were to elapse before educators finally found the right tone to capture a child's interest – until the *New Education*'s liberating influence took up and adapted Rousseau's ideas at the end of the nineteenth century. A new generation of liberators emerged with Maria Montessori, Dewey, Decorly, Bakulés and Claparède, and the genius of these innovators, their theories and their methods of teaching young children to read gave Paul Faucher the idea of editing a collection for children between the age of three and ten – *Albums du Père Castor* – of which he published over three hundred from 1927 to 1967. They are primarily educative albums, each one having a particular educative aim while forming part of a wider scheme which must be seen as a whole to be understood and put to good use by the teacher. The *Père Castor* albums are designed to help children to master the mechanisms of reading and to understand clearly and precisely what they read; they are presented with a familiar but exciting vision of the world which satisfies and stimulates their minds and their senses. Here, then, is a series of publications which entertains while educating and is worth classifying as children's literature.

What are the principles on which the *Père Castor* albums are based? The first principle is to avoid forming a stereotyped

5. For Bakulé see Adolphe Ferrière: *Trois pionniers de l'éducation nouvelle* (Flammarion).

response in the young reader. Adults often create a dull, mechanical relationship between children and their books. To begin with, books are often too heavy to be held comfortably; they are therefore opened on a table before the child whose eyes follow in a regular clockwork movement the no less regular rows of little black signs which his mind labours to decipher, while a more or less relevant picture occasionally breaks the monotony. Paul Faucher wanted to break away from this format; children, he decided, must not be compelled to sit still while they read, children's books should involve the child in the same relationship as any other plaything. Therefore he reduced his books to album-size and did away with hard covers; the booklets were easy to handle, neither too large nor too small, and each one had an immediate individuality thanks to the variety of colours, pictures and typography on the covers. Inside, the type was irregular but well-balanced and led the reader's eye along curves that, although apparently haphazard were, in fact, related both to the rhythm of sentences and the visual and breathing capacities of the reader. The typographical pattern is generously illustrated and the pictures complement the text, telling the story in another idiom, explaining or filling it out. Each *Père Castor* album offers the reader a surprise trip; sometimes the text takes the lead, sometimes the illustrations, but they are always interrelated. Some albums must be played instead of read – or rather they can be read only in the context of a game; these are the 'game' books for cutting out, taking to pieces and putting together, matching text with illustrations in a variety of combinations.[6] In this way reading becomes an activity which involves the child's powers of observation, his initiative and his imagination as well as the usual faculties. When Paul Faucher published the

6. Cf. the albums published between 1930–37 by *Père Castor*'s original team, Nathalie Parrain, Bellenfant and Angèle Malclés: *L'Atelier d'Arlequin, Album fée, Crayons et ciseaux, Ribambelles, Allons vite, Chez nous il y a* ... etc.

first album he was well ahead of his time, and publishers of children's books all over the world are indebted to his ingenuity.7

Mention should here be made of the Czech educationist Havranek[8] whose methods of teaching writing and arithmetic were invaluable to Paul Faucher's innovations.

The second principle concerns story-telling, which should be based on actual experience and not on bookish, abstract knowledge; it must avoid, therefore, allusions, reminiscences, literary comparisons, indirect speech and generalizations: it must, on the contrary, use a direct, positive style and evocative language. As subject-matter, *Père Castor* provides the child with a plot he can master because it is about real life, essential, primary activities (playing, laughing, moving, exercising one's limbs) and can be seen as all-embracing. He rejects subjects which are too closely related to social or economic conditions or to a conventional, and therefore relative, moral code. He concentrates on outdoor life, where the same gestures and the same basic activities recur; protagonists are more often animals than children – who would require too precise and specific a social background. Young readers will find themselves intellectually at ease and emotionally satisfied with such reading-matter. They can follow the story without ever being upset or antagonized by overstimulation. *Père Castor* does not attempt to enthrall the imagination; the shadow of uncertainty or doubt that lingers after a book has been read seems to him to be a two-edged weapon where young children are concerned. The stories he publishes leave no impression on the mind except by stimulating play; they promote activity, not

7. There is a revival of interest in France in the educational uses of this sort of 'activity' book. The emphasis is now more on the outside world and the environment of today. The best of the publishers exploring this field is 'L'École des loisirs'.

8. Havranek: *Les cinq doigts de la main, La clé de l'ecriture et du dessin* (Flammarion, 1953).

day-dreaming, as in the typical example of *Le Panier qui venait de la mer*.

The *Père Castor* albums can be roughly divided into three groups: albums for very young children catering for the need for activity. By encouraging creative games, they help children to become aware of themselves and explore their capabilities. Among these are *Les Enfants-chats*, *La Vache orange*, *Quand Coulicoco dort* . . . such books speak a language children can 'understand' and to which they can 'respond', as Rousseau would say. The second group is nature albums which place the child in familiar surroundings, where he knows what is happening. In this particular area it is difficult to improve on *Père Castor*: he pioneered the genre with *Roman des bêtes*, *Montreur d'images* and the ones that tell the story of a natural cycle in the form of an anecdote such as *Perlette goutte d'eau* or *Conte de la marguerite*. In the last group are albums portraying children and dramatizing everyday events, notably those by Marie Colmont and Albertine Deletaille. Here we are no longer concerned with recognizing and identifying or with introducing children to the natural order of things. But *Père Castor* seems to have failed to achieve his aim, which was simply to hold the reader's attention. Marie Colmont and Albertine Deletaille's stories are perfectly balanced self-contained tales but – perhaps as a result – they are not adventurous enough for an eight-year-old's fancy. The characters are basically too static to be exciting. Their childhood state is never threatened, so they never risk losing their composure; they never grow up and it seems most unlikely that they ever could; children they are and children they will remain – and glad of it. But a real child's desperate need for emotional security is always balanced by an equally imperative need to be free and though this conflict is forcefully expressed in many a folk tale where children are lost and in distress but, miraculously, fend for themselves, it never appears to trouble the *Père*

Castor heroes. They are spared that desire – so natural to all children – with its attendant fears and apprehensions, to be grown up.

Restricted by a standard format and a limited number of pages, but more by his overall concept, *Père Castor* is incapable of involving his young readers in the fate of another child because every story, even Tom Thumb's, requires its share of mystery. Moreover, these children, like those created by Madame de Genlis and Berquin, are there only to prove some educational point. Because education has changed, they are now active, resourceful and generous, where they used to be docile, reasonable and charitable, but they are never pathetic or – alas – amusing; for that they would have to possess the contradictions they so badly lack.

Père Castor's experiment is unique. None of the attempts at educational publications which immediately preceded or followed it has ever attained a similar continuity and consistency of output. Among the more successful, however, are the stories Leo Tolstoy wrote to be read in class. Concerning their style and purpose he said:

Many people, and especially children, ask themselves whenever they read a story, if the subject is probable; if they decide that it is not they say: it is just something made up, it isn't true. People who judge in this way are wrong. Truth will not be revealed to those who are content with the knowledge that a certain event has taken place or might take place, but to those who understand *what life should be*.

Truth will not be revealed by the story-teller who describes how things happened, what one person or another did, but by the story-teller who shows how men do good or evil ... There are stories, fables, allegories and legends where fabulous events are described that have never happened and never will happen and yet which are true because they show where the highest truth can be found.

Novels, too, can take a child's moral development as their

theme. Among the more interesting are *Milo* by Charles Vildrac and *Le Drôle* by François Mauriac in France; *Pollyanna* by Eleanor Porter, *Betsy* by Dorothy Canfield Fisher, *Little Women* and *Good Wives* by Louisa May Alcott in the U.S.A. Their only shortcoming is that no really memorable hero or heroine emerges from any of these. Happy people are not interesting and Vildrac's *Milo*, for example, is perfectly happy and well-balanced. The victim of a totally misguided education is more likely to appeal to our sympathy; thus Drôle, who is as spoilt as a child can be, is often amusing, although sometimes unconvincing. Little Rose's deliverance from her former worries and her attainment of freedom in *Eight Cousins* is also entertaining, but there is a world of difference between the young reader's cold appraisal of such edifying novels and real enthusiasm.

What, then, do children read if they turn up their noses at the books written expressly for them? What did the eighteenth-century child, sated with edifying, instructive literature, read on the sly? We have the answer precisely from one of these books, *Les Veillées du château* by Madame de Genlis:

'What are you reading?' asked Madame de Clemire.
'Mother ... it is ... *Prince Percinet et Princesse Gracieuse.*'
'A fairy tale! How can such reading-matter interest you?'
'Mother, I know it's wrong of me; but I must admit that I like fairy tales ... !'

3. *Once Upon a Time*

Possibly all genuine children's literature is a survival of the folk tales and legends which feature in every civilization. At some point the story-teller's wide, heterogeneous audience disintegrates; adults have no time to listen to stories – there are more pressing things to be done. As the story loses its social function women replace men as story-tellers, the story becomes an old wives' tale and its audience, no longer a cross-section of the community actively participating, is composed exclusively of children who listen spellbound to a grandmother figure – or to Mother Goose. The stories come to be the accepted preserve of children and it was, therefore, for them that a modern anthologist such as Perrault collected and retold the tales 'which our ancestors invented for their children'.[1] Perrault stressed the connection between children and folk tales still further when he published *Histoires ou contes du temps passé avec des moralités*, this time under the name of his nineteen-year-old son Pierre Darmencour – whom certain scholars claim to have been their real author.[2] In Germany too, Clemens Brentano's *Tales for Children* and the Brothers Grimm's *Household Tales* collections were explicitly directed at children, while

1. Perrault, *Contes en vers* (1695), preface to the fourth edition.
2. For this suggestion as well as for an interpretation of the *Contes* see Marc Soriano's thesis: *Les Contes de Perrault, culture savante et tradition populaire*, Gallimard, Paris, 1963.

Newbery's little books brought the image of Mother Goose surrounded by children into practically every English home.

It seems to be generally acknowledged that children are fond of fairy tales and therefore that fairy tales are for children. Yet strangely enough, we are told that to indulge this taste is a serious educational error; children often do not know what is good for them – indeed they can dote on things that are positively harmful. According to certain pedagogues fairy tales are precisely the most unsuitable form of literature for children, and, therefore, enlightened adults who know what children really need, have always been extremely suspicious of fairy tales.

This attitude hardens when we go from oral to written literature. The earliest books actually intended for children were not – or only very rarely as in the case of Newbery's publications – tales drawn from a tradition that really appealed to them, but so-called edifying works. Even when children's books were not purely didactic and moralizing but tried to amuse, even when they merged with the general trend of popular literature, they actually borrowed much less from folklore than might be expected. For instance, pedlar's pamphlets or chapbooks which made free use of folk tales, never reproduced them faithfully, but retained only the more colourful aspects of local custom and discarded the magic.

The first genuine collections of folk tales were not really written for children; although Perrault and the Brothers Grimm used children more or less as an excuse for their tales – and even, in the case of Perrault, spoke in their name – they were, in fact, addressing the adult. These collections, officially labelled for children, sought to impart a message of wisdom and enlightenment to a wide adult audience. Though the motives for the folklore revival in the different countries of Europe and in America may vary greatly, this pattern always recurs: the tales are first told by adults to children and subsequently borrowed from children for adult consumption; suddenly, but with unerring regularity, this primitive, unsophisticated literature becomes the object of general interest and of serious scholarly consideration. Germans, Scandinavians and Russians have possibly been among the more enthusiastic delvers into their folk tradition from which they hoped to derive a new, yet essentially 'national' vigour for their respective cultures. There is a time in the evolution of every nation when it will seek to assert its specific identity by means of folklore.

In Europe, the earliest collections of tales directly derived from folklore were probably Italian. *Le Piacevoli Notti* (1550–1553) by Straporola and *Lo Cunto de li Cunti* (1634–1636) by Basile have been seen as the sources for Perrault's translations.[3] Though they follow the basic archetypal themes, the verbal virtuosity and wealth of ornamentation and burlesque which lends them a sophisticated and – in the case of Basile at least – a baroque charm, deprives them of the original limpidity and directness of the spoken word. The true folk tale, the 'fiaba' survived only in the countryside and was not transcribed till much later. Perrault was, for a long time, the only writer in Europe capable of capturing the intonation of the oral tale.

However, where the Italians stressed licentious elements, Perrault, on the contrary, brought out the morality, although the two things are, in fact, only facets of an identical feature. In Perrault's version the tales are expressions of popular common sense; they provide amusing examples of tricks played on the Lord of the Manor, of masculine brutality towards women and of the subterfuges used by women to avoid such treatment. He allows his characters enough freedom of action to manipulate social conventions to their advantage – with the result that in the end these conventions are more firmly established, for our ancestors, '. . . always

3. Cf. Marc Soriano, op cit.

took great care to give their tales a virtuous and edifying moral conclusion. Virtue was always rewarded and vice punished. The fact that it is worthwhile being honest, patient, prudent, hard-working and obedient was always brought to the fore as well as the consequences of transgressing such rules . . . '.4

Infallible precepts and rules of conduct are equally suitable for little children and for the lower classes of society if they are to be preserved from evil. They can also be appreciated by 'discerning persons' who will see therein a proof of their own righteousness. Eroticism is frowned on and the 'moral conclusions' are both enlightening and cautionary as, for example, in the French version of *Little Red Riding Hood*:

> Here we see how young children
> – and particularly young ladies
> who are pretty, graceful and sweet –
> should always beware of strangers
> and how, indeed, it is small wonder
> if the wolf devours so many.
> But when I say 'the wolf' you must understand
> that all wolves are not of one ilk;
> there are those with endearing ways
> gentle, friendly, apparently kind,
> who, obliging, soft-spoken and genial
> escort young ladies to their doorstep (or further).
> But alas, these mealy-mouthed monsters
> are more to be feared than the others!

This simple tale with its unsophisticated imagery, brutal concision of action and primordial terrors entirely preserved, was turned into an edifying rhyme for 'young ladies'.

Such interpretations and adjustments of folk tales to make them fit the social conventions of their age were taken even further after Perrault. The crude, peasant idiom of the originals was replaced by abstract, elegant phrases: from the

4. Perrault, Preface to *Contes en vers*, fourth edition (1695).

vernacular 'Lift the latch and come in'[5] sentimental verse
was substituted:

> Oh blue bird colour of time
> Come quickly, fly to my call[6]

Perrault's successors disguised the old folk themes in
flounces of fine speech and recast them in drawing-room
rhetoric to conform to the political and social attitudes of
the Monarchy's latter years. *Le cabinet des fées*, for instance,
was a reflection of contemporary society; the original
skeleton was there, but strangely clothed. This is not to deny
the outstanding poetic qualities of the best of these stories –
Madame Leprince de Beaumont's *Beauty and the Beast* and
Madame d'Aulnoy's *Les contes des fées*, for example – but the
elements of folklore in them are used only as a framework
for intricate literary symbolism. This metamorphosis was
made all the easier because symbolic tales rely heavily on all
kinds of pretences and disguises. Eroticism in folk tales is
commonly hidden under a complex symbolism very similar
to that of dreams; folk tales also frequently juggle with
moral and social values in a disguised form and thus may
appear to express the most deeply felt aspirations of the
society that produced them.

During this time the form of the tale did not remain
static, for writers adopted all kinds of literary conventions
such as the pastoral, the comedy or verse tale. In the second
half of the eighteenth century, when fairy tales became
fashionable in France, the evolution of the folk tale can be
distinctly traced. Masque and fancy dress invaded both
literature and painting, and oriental costumes enjoyed a
wide popularity. Galland's translation of the *Thousand and
One Nights* between 1704 and 1717 was a revelation. He had,
indeed, watered down these cruel, erotic stories and turned

5. Perrault, *Le Petit Chaperon Rouge* (Little Red Riding-Hood).
6. Madame D'Aulnoy, *L'Oiseau bleu.*

them into gallant romances, but Arabian vigour is not easily quelled and the oriental splendour of the subject-matter was enhanced rather than otherwise by the affected elegance of the translation. Oriental tales opened up a treasury of new ideas for the old themes; magic objects, enchanted places and a range of startling transformations quite different from the unobtrusive, almost logical metamorphoses of western convention. Perrault's pumpkin does indeed turn into a coach, but there is nothing absolutely improbable about such a thing – some writers have even seen it as 'Cartesian'.[7] One does not, however, expect people to turn into animals quite so readily and our supernatural beings – ogres, witches, fairies etc. – were hardly more than a superior form of humanity and had no striking characteristics to put them definitely into the realm of the monstrous. One of the first tales in the *Thousand and One Nights*, on the other hand, begins with these words: 'Know, Great Prince of the Genies, that we are three brothers: two are black dogs which you see before you, I myself am the third . . . '[8] Only in eastern tales, Arabian, Russian, Ukranian etc. does real magic play a part; metamorphosis is an everyday occurrence; living creatures spring from bits and pieces at an 'Abracadabra', objects have weird attributes – castles are enchanted, huts run on chicken's legs.

Once the treasure-trove had been sorted out and adapted, children began to lose interest while sophisticated adult readers found it more and more to their taste. What the eighteenth-century adult read into these tales was social allegory: the mutual dependence and ambivalent relationship of rich and poor, men and women; he could not conceive that they might portray different, less clear-cut and more intangible moods. However, the German romantics of the

7. Cf. Marc Soriano's critique of this interpretation, op. cit.

8. *Thousand and One Nights*, the 'Tale of the Second Aged Man and the Two Black Dogs'.

Sturm und Drang period were to find another message in the folk tale. The folk tale, according to Herder, bears 'the last vestiges of a people's beliefs, intuitive sense, creative energy and instinctive behaviour; it comes from a stage of consciousness in which men dreamt what they did not know, believed what they could not see and in which a man's actions involved his whole being because it was still untouched by any cultural influence'. By now the tale no longer expressed homely wisdom in simple language; the story-teller had lost the role of teacher that Perrault had given him and had become anonymous; his story was not the expression of a particular society but of a whole people, a people 'still untouched by any cultural influence'. The tale was now a truly national phenomenon and, as such, could be used to instil a sense of national identity. To nineteenth-century Europe, torn by nationalist revolutions in which Germans, Italians and Slavs were trying to overthrow arbitrary political frontiers and establish themselves as nations, each with a common heritage, folklore appeared as a touchstone and a catalyst. Through their folklore these scattered exiles could rediscover their identity and draw close together. The folk revival in German and Russian music and in literature is a proof of this. The earliest collections published were *Volksmärchen der Deutschen* by J.-K.-A. Musäus, and *Kindermärchen* and *Rheinmärchen* by Clemens Brentano, followed by *Kinder und Hausmärchen* by the Brothers Grimm: this last was the first systematic, scholarly anthology and children's writers today still find it a source of inspiration. To these forerunners may be added Pushkin's collections in Russia and, much later, those of Afanassiev, not to mention the remarkable collection by Asbjørnsen and Moe in Norway – *Norwegian Tales*.

Ethnic minorities could at last make themselves heard, could employ their own splendidly naïve idiom to express a brilliance and earthiness which no written literature had yet had a chance to trivialize. Random but characteristic examples are the Flemish *Contes d'un buveur de bière* and *Contes du roi Gambrinus* by Charles Deulin; the Louisiana Negro, *Uncle Remus* by Joel Chandler Harris, and a Baltic collection, *Contes lithuaniens de Ma Mère l'Oye* by Oscar-Vladimir de L. Milosz. All are outstanding for the liveliness of their stories and the narrative skill, integrity and invention of the story-teller.

The increasing seriousness and thoroughness of research re-established the natural vigour of folk tradition; its epic qualities were recognized and its symbolism, freed from rationalization, recovered its emotional validity; the story is simplified, and its dreamlike qualities are revealed. However, the invisible pendulum which swings inexorably from a child audience to an adult audience and back to children again, now swung the folk tale back. Once the tale's ancestry had been rediscovered and its roots in the collective unconscious had been unearthed, the great anthologists, from the Brothers Grimm onwards, associated children with their publications. Joel Chandler Harris's old Negro tells his tales to 'Miss Sally's little boy', Blaise Cendrars collected *Petits Contes nègres pour les enfants des blancs*, and Milosz presented *Contes lithuaniens de Ma Mère l'Oye* to French children. Children are, incontestably, more responsive to the appeal of popular tradition than adults, but the pendulum cannot be halted. Having come back to its child audience the folk tale gradually underwent a change. Infantilism and insipidity crept in, and themes in which a degree of explanation is implicit, such as the ordeal or trial, took over. In fact, the trial was identified with work, and pattern was no longer mainly rhythmical but was charged with a moral content – idleness punished and work rewarded – as in the classic story of the *Three Little Pigs*. When the themes were restricted and exploited, the stories lost their natural imagery, becoming nothing but mechanical exercises.

Animal stories are particularly prone to this treatment because the conflicts are simple and predictable. We are shown the tricks rabbits, foxes, turtle-doves, wolves and nanny-goats play on each other; repeated in book after book the story becomes increasingly lifeless. Only verbal skill can save such stories,[9] and here dialect is better than the received language. A language like Russian, with a rich, musical vocabulary that lends itself to bold experimentation, and one with limited resources and unobtrusive harmonies, like French, show up the differences even more.

Even watered down, the folk tale still has some surprises in store, especially when it is told to very young children. One children's writer who realized this, Sara Cone Bryant, with *How to Tell Stories to our Children* introduced folklore to the American kindergarten. This was a difficult undertaking; it required an unerring educational insight and the sensitivity to pick out from the vast amount of material the stories which might spark off a four-year-old's imagination. Not many authors were as successful as Miss Bryant, which makes Margaret Wise Brown's adaptations in America and Natha Caputo's *Contes des quatre vents* in France, doubly valuable.[10]

This shows that one of the folk tale's characteristics is that its structure is constant, but can be expressed in various forms according to the psycho-cultural needs of the moment. Van Gennep observes that identical themes are presented, 'sometimes as myths, sometimes as legends and sometimes as tales, depending on the period, the material circumstances and on any social change ... If economic or intellectual conditions alter, the theme passes from one of these conventions to another. It is not that it has degenerated;

9. Or parody, as in Tomi Ungerer's anti-stories which the author illustrates himself with great verve.

10. See Oh-Ryen Seung's admirable, *Psycho-pédagogie du conte, essai suivi de seize contes coréens*, Fleurus, Paris, 1971.

it has changed its significance, no more.'[11] Such a change of form may also correspond to purely educational motives. Thus a theme like 'The Abandoned Princess' can be told as *Patient Griselda* or as *Geneviève de Brabant*, becoming an anecdote or an illustration of historical custom depending on whether tales are intended as recreation or instruction. This is a theme like the Swan Maiden which has been told in every country all over the world as far apart as Polynesia and Russia, sometimes appearing as a myth, often as a fairy story and even as an anecdote belonging to the times of our ancestors. The story of Psyche, whose curiosity to see the husband who visits her only under cover of dark ruins her marriage, is a slightly unusual form of this theme in that the roles of the sexes are reversed. The story of the prince who captures one of a group of 'swan' maidens, as in *The Nine Peahens and the Golden Apples*, reappears under many different titles, and the idea of the humans who spend part of their life as birds is repeated in Hans Andersen's *The Wild Swans*. The story appears again as the folk tale which explains some natural phenomenon in the Shetland and Hebridean Islands, where it is not unusual to find a Scottish family attributing certain characteristics to the fact that long, long ago an ancestor married a seal woman who returned to the sea when she discovered the seal skin which had been hidden by her husband when he captured her. Matthew Arnold's well-known *Forsaken Merman* is another example of the treatment of the same theme.

If the fairy tale satisfies a basic psychological need – freedom, wish-fulfilment – the legend integrates the child into his society. The educationally-minded anthologist, therefore, selects tales which have a social or political implication and help the child to adapt to his background by providing codes of behaviour as well as a national mythology. Examples of such national legends are those of King Arthur

11. Van Gennep, *La Formation des légendes*, Flammarion, Paris, 1920.

or Charlemagne – the hero who, after mighty deeds, sleeps in some remote cave, only to wake when his country is in desperate need of his services once more. This sort of anthologist will tend to omit the simple fairy tale or traditional folk tales and, since the seventeenth century, anthologies have favoured the legend. A list of such publications proves the point. In the *Bibliothèque bleue* of 1660 we find *La Légende de Richard sans peur*, *Robert le Diable*, *Grisélidis* and *Geneviève de Brabant*. In 1703 James Boswell listed in *Curious Productions* the chapbooks he had enjoyed as a child; these were *Jack the Giantkiller*, *The Seven Champions of Christendom*, *Count Guy of Warwick*, *The King and the Cobbler*, *Sir Richard Whittington*, *Johnny Armstrong of Westmoreland*, *The Babes in the Wood* and *The Friar and the Boy* – in other words an equal proportion of tales and legends. This is more or less the pattern of a popular modern collection such as *Contes et légendes*[12] – a modernized, better-balanced and more scientific version of the *Bibliothèque bleue* or the chapbooks. Significantly enough, among the first publications in this series are legends from Greece and Rome – the foundations of our bourgeois culture. They were popularized outside the classroom to sanction that code of reference known as the humanities, whose ethics Paul Valéry denounced: 'The vague, baroque notion of the humanities was instituted by Louis Philippe. An essentially *bourgeois* ideal for people who want to establish a class'.[13]

Recent educational trends have given the series new impetus and scope – the humanities, ethnology – the discovery of the third world, etc. The folk tale is being redirected towards extra-scholastic ends and is becoming a means of conditioning the future citizen to current social values rather than of imaginative inspiration. The child who

12. Ed. Fernand Nathan. The first title in this series – *Légendes et contes d'Alsace* – appeared in 1913.

13. Paul Valéry, *Cahiers*, XXIII, 1940

reads these books is shown himself in his historical and geographical background and also finds a curious nationalistic fervour that seems totally out of place nowadays, especially in a series of books designed to have universal appeal. In the volume *Contes et légendes des Flandres*, the author wishes to show that the French are still one united people even though their political opinions may differ. He addresses his hero – who has been royalist, republican and bonapartist in succession – as follows: ' . . . at dusk, take your big stick and walk along those childhood canals. Recall for us, Bernard, your distant youth and your anonymous but great achievements, recall your part in the making of France. Stand still for a moment and let us look at you . . . '14

Substantially abridged versions of masterpieces which are part of every sixth-former's stock in trade, also find a place in these volumes: *Contes et légendes tirées des opéras célèbres, de Racine, de Corneille, de Shakespeare.* There are also digests of four or so literary works which are supposed to give one the minimum necessary understanding of a foreign culture – what an educated man should be able to discuss offhand whenever the subject comes up in conversation.15 *Contes et légendes* sums up, moreover, with useful hints to its readers on respectable occupations mentioning as examples well-known writers: ' . . . If later on you would like to be better acquainted with the spirit of Mexico and with its past, you might study ethnology at the *Musée de l'homme* and even, some day, perhaps write a scholarly treatise like those by Professor Rivet or Jacques Soustelle.'16 How tempting it sounds!

It would be wrong to expound at length on a collection

14. Antonia de Lauwereyens de Roösendaàle, 'L'un d'eux' in *Contes et légendes des Flandres*, Fernand Nathan, Paris, 1963.

15 *Contes et légendes d'Espagne*, F. Nathan, Paris.

16. Robert Escarpit, preface to *Contes et légendes de Mexique*.

that seems a caricature of all the faults of the French education system, but the series is uniquely characteristic of its
genre. Because it has lasted for so long and is so well known
it is the only one that offers its readers such a wide range of
'stories' and 'legends'. Comparison with Andrew Lang's
collections (*The Blue Fairy Book* etc.) shows up its frustrating
limitations. There is nothing narrow or pedantic about
Lang's books, although they are obviously the work of a
scholar and humanist, and they have given and will continue
to give immense pleasure to generations of children.

Of course, when legends pass from the scholar's pen to
the poet's they immediately regain their sparkle. Kipling's
Puck of Pook's Hill (1906) is perhaps the only example of an
unashamedly didactic work that presents a selfish, inward-
looking morality, and yet possesses a very real charm that
does not entirely depend on Kipling's linguistic skill.
Kipling was most certainly a master – or rather a magician –
of language. When one turns the pages of this wonderfully
evocative book to discover England's past in incidents
which, though meant to instruct, are so transformed by
the author's imaginative power, one forgets the didacticism
and exclaims: yes, this is life, this is how it happened, just
like this and not in any other way. For example, nothing
could be more natural than the dialogue between the
writer's children and the Norman Knights or the young
Roman centurion.

The realm of real magic is restricted: in France, the history
of the fairy tale evolves from Perrault through the *Cabinet
des fées* to the oriental legend. Every child knows the stories,
though they usually reach him in abridged versions and
adorned with second-rate illustrations.

Pastiche is a danger for contemporary writers. For some
reason it seems to be assumed that any story can be dressed
up as a fairy tale. Old themes are served up again and again
under two guises. Madame d'Aulnoy's method is to pile on

the decorative trimmings whereas Jean Macé trims them down to serve the ends of education – the lesson of the good child rewarded.[17] And if nobody reads Jean Macé and Madame d'Aulnoy any longer, it cannot be said that their modern emulators are more popular.

One successful attempt in France at writing modern fairy tales is Madame de Ségur's *Nouveaux Contes de fées*. She borrowed some of the main themes of folklore, such as prohibitions and trials, in *Bon petit Henri*, forbidden fruit and transformations in *Blandine*, the outcast sister in *Princesse Rosette*, Beauty and the Beast in *Ourson* and managed to re-create the incantatory spell of the oral tale and its uncanny atmosphere. Hers is an exceptional example of tales consciously inspired from folklore where the symbols do not appear arbitrary and lose their hold on the imagination. This established framework seems to suit Madame de Ségur very well; she does not find it constricting and cleverly adapts her own set of symbols to it. Moreover, in *Nouveaux Contes de fées* the reader accepts without demur magical objects, conventional places and strange beings; good or bad fairies, talking animals and spirits assert themselves as things which exist and cannot be denied, but, like reality itself, they are inexplicable and mysterious. Madame de Ségur's repressed sensuality seems to have intensified her five senses – particularly that of taste – and enabled her to create a whole system of sensory correspondences that adds a tremendous vitality to her writing and her imagery. For instance, in the description of Princess Rosette's ornaments, her fairy godmother has given her a necklace of hazelnuts, a bracelet of dried beans and a brooch of medlars; but when Rosette puts them on to go to the ball they turn into pearls, rubies, diamonds and carbuncles 'as big as nuts', 'hazelnuts' or 'pears'. Treasure as an idea has a strong fascination for children, who love to hoard useless sparkling odds and ends

17. *Contes du petit château*, Hetzel, 1862.

in secret. In this story, precious stones glitter like fire and are cold as ice so that they appeal both to the eye and to the touch; they are compared to fruit and thus make the reader's mouth water . . . this detailed description which recurs three times in the tale, is remarkably effective and leaves an indelible impression on the memory.

Apart from these stories, the modern fairy tale has definitely had its day.* At present the folk tale has almost vanished from children's literature – except for a few stories about talking animals in books for very young children and these owe their popularity less to their subject-matter than to their form. From the opening words 'Once upon a time . . . ' children are on familiar ground, they know where they stand and where they are going; they are prepared to be led by magic numbers through enchanted landscapes and dark forests, encountering adventures and tricks till the happy ending. It is, therefore, astonishing, almost shocking, when a story starts with the words 'Now look out! We're going to begin. When we've come to the end of this part we shall know more than we do now'. This isn't playing the game, it is breaking all the established rules, and yet this is how one of the best known story-tellers begins – Hans Andersen in *The Snow Queen*!

* Editor's note: There are some modern writers who have managed to transmute the ancient magic into modern terms. Examples of this are E. Nesbit's longer books (not her short fairy stories which tend to be too jocular). Also the writing of Lucy Boston, Mary Norton, and Joan Aitken's shorter stories. These writers deal seriously with magic which is one of the hallmarks of the 'true' fairy story.

4. *Hans Christian Andersen or Reality*

It may seem paradoxical to say that Hans Andersen's stories are not folk tales. His links with folklore are obvious and he was, indeed, greatly indebted to this tradition whose poetry, he believed, was reborn like the Phoenix rising from its own ashes when it renewed contact with the people from whom it had sprung:

... a little bird, the most exquisite of song-birds; it sang with the ringing voice of the thrush, the throbbings of a human heart and the echoes of distant lands which beckon to birds of passage. The song-bird flew over hills and dales, fields and woods; it was the bird of folk poetry which cannot die.[1]

When Hans Andersen called his autobiography *The Tale of My Life* he was seeing himself as the hero of a fairy tale. From under the mask of the ugly duckling peeps the face of the despised brother but, like Aladdin – another tale which always obsessed him – Hans Andersen, finally acknowledged by society, ended by riding in the king's carriage through the streets of his native village. He saw himself living a fairy tale, and how right he was, even though, unlike a fairy story, his love affairs had no happy ending: his own life story remained unfinished. This was perhaps one of the most singular features of this most singular of men, that he never had a partner; his dreams of

1. The Bird of Folk Poetry, in *Tales from Hans Andersen*.

love were never realized, but lived only in his memories – a handful of letters or the face of an unfaithful little sweetheart whose picture he treasured all his life. Apart from these imaginary loves, his writing, his intense though rather superficial friendships and his numerous social commitments, what was the true life of Hans Christian Andersen? Who was he?

Two words sum up his genius and his fate: story-teller and traveller. In one of his earliest tales, *Thumbelina*, we are introduced to the 'man who knows how to tell stories'. Later comes the 'student' who can tell so many tales and cuts out long paper chains of little figures to amuse the children; then there is the 'old gentleman' or the 'Godfather' who enchants them with his picture book. He was a story-teller by vocation, which is not surprising when one thinks that he could not read or write till he was fifteen and all his learning was self-taught. His vivid imagination having had no other outlet than the spoken word, he naturally continued to express himself in the familiar popular idiom, and speech always preceded writing for him. His earlier tales were *told* in a rather hackneyed style in which he obviously felt safe, but he gradually came to rely more on his own imagination and gifts of perception and punctuated his writing with the interjections, exclamations, twists and turns, outbursts and repetitions which make his descriptions captivating.

The fact that he was a story-teller dictated his choice of audience. Hans Andersen wanted to be a children's writer, but he did not allow this to compromise his literary aims. Referring to *Little Ida's Flowers* he wrote: 'The story-teller's voice must be heard in the style. This means that the writing must be as near as possible to speech. The tale may be for children, but it must be understood by adults as well'. Of *The Little Mermaid* he said: 'Had I published it on its own it would have seemed more ambitious, therefore I thought it better to include it in the group of tales I had begun; those which precede it are perhaps more suited to children than this one, which can only be fully appreciated by adults. However, I hope and trust that children will enjoy it and that they will be moved by it and will accept even the ending quite naturally.' His first stories were simple transcriptions of tales he had heard as a child: *The Tinder Box*, *Big Claus and Little Claus*, *The Princess and the Pea*, *The Emperor's New Clothes*, *The Wild Swans*. Among them, however, is a tale of his own invention, a fantasy inspired by a conversation with a little girl: *Little Ida's Flowers*. Hans Andersen later freed himself altogether from the constrictions of folklore. His second collection was called *Adventures for Children* and then simply *Tales*.

From the very beginning Hans Andersen was more than a mere anthologist. He used the folk tale as a loose framework for his early stories but often exploded its conventions, especially its stock of endings. The folk tale never follows life's unpredictable, fanciful and irreversible pattern; it corrects, compensates and inevitably contrives reassuring endings. Hans Andersen's tales, on the other hand, never try to reassure; they offer no outlet to desire, no concessions to wishful thinking, and do not redress the balance of life. He does not lead his heroes to their destination but leaves them to wander as best they can towards a goal they may never reach. In a fairy story the peasant-prince as in Grimm's *King Thrushbeard* or the outcast brother as in *Ivan the Ninny* may finally marry the princess; but Hans Andersen's swineherd refuses to do so.

And with that he went into his Kingdom, shut the door and bolted it; but she could stand outside if she cared to and sing:
>Ach du lieber Augustin
>Alles ist Voek, Voek, Voek!

The tune ends on a note that echoes in the imagination with the sadness of a future beyond human control. Thus *The*

Swineherd is an anti-story where real time, fluid and unpredictable, takes the place of mythical time and this is the poet's first step towards the conquest of reality.

From then on Hans Andersen tried, in one tale after another, to distinguish between the folk tale and the story and to establish their different forms: *Little Ida's Flowers, The Snow Queen, a folk tale in seven parts, The Wind tells the Story of Valdemar Daa and his Daughters, Willie Winkie, The Elder Mother*. His whole output may be seen as an exercise in the art of the narrative, in the various ways of telling a story. He invites the reader to share the exercise and participate in the story. In a single tale we find different paces in the narrative and different depths of imagination. The first and also one of the most successful of this kind is *Little Ida's Flowers*. The flowers' adventures arise from a conversation between Ida and the student but the story escapes from the story-teller (is acted) and opens out before Ida's gaze as she watches, now a mere spectator, the ball which ends in the flowers' dying. Can one speak of an ending, however, when the story merges into the game of the flowers' funeral to which Ida invites her cousins? The game is only another way of story-telling.

The story-teller comes into his stories as student, as God-father, but especially in the enigmatic guise of the traveller. Hans Andersen's whole life was a journey in which he held briefly passing events and emotions. All transitory things – seasons, birds, leaves, the wind – have something to say, a message to impart:

Hu-woosh! Let's be off! Let's be off!
And winter whirled along; winter, and summer, they whirled along – and still whirl, as I whirl, as the snow drifts, and the apple blossom drifts and the leaves fall. Let's be off, off, off! And mankind with us![2]

2. *The Wind tells the Story of Valdemar Daa and his Daughters.*

In folk tales the hero sets out 'to seek his fortune'; the goal is never more definite than that and in Andersen's early stories the wanderers are aimless, too: 'Hi, there, my friend, where are you off to?' 'Out into the wide world . . .'3 But the meaning of these wanderings gradually emerges: the bird, the leaf and the story-teller himself are in search of a story; they set out 'into the wide world' to look for stories. Tales are to be found in the most unexpected places, in the heart of a rose or in the eye of a needle and when they are recognized, they transform the most commonplace objects into something magical. 'A story may have knocked on our door and gone unnoticed and unwelcomed. I am off into the world to find it!'4 How can we recognize a story? What is the gift that makes mere talk fall into place and become a story? How does a story with its characters and its pattern emerge from a jumble of words or ideas suggested by the wind, a leaf, a bird, perhaps something mentioned idly by a child, or by the story-teller himself? The answer is a sudden flash of perception about the nature of an object. The thing itself will not necessarily take first place in the story – the teapot, the tin soldier, the rose or the pea – it is more likely simply to be the thing that sparks off the story-teller's imagination, setting the creative mechanism in motion – the flowers on the balcony in *The Shadow*, the window-boxes on the roof in *The Snow Queen*. Simply to see the thing is not always enough to give birth to a story, sometimes it must be touched as well; 'Mother says that everything you look at becomes a fairy tale and that everything you touch turns into a story' says the little sick boy to his old neighbour in *Elm-Tree Mother*. Here the sensuous nature of inspiration is emphasized by the mention of 'touch'. Hans Andersen was

3. *The Travelling Companion.*
4. *The Will-o-the-Wisp is in the Town.* This story is only very rarely included in editions of Hans Andersen's stories and for this reason has been added as an appendix at the end of this book.

was not given to abstract visions. He was not obsessed by strange imaginary worlds like Blake or Poe, nor did he see things in a haze, emerging from mists or artistically blurred: he saw them clearly, and to make doubly sure of their real existence he went right up to them and touched them. A man becomes a poet when seeing things in their total reality, as though he had been short-sighted and had put on a pair of spectacles for the first time: 'I see everything so clearly, I feel so bright and intelligent,' says the clerk turned poet under the spell of the *Goloshes of Fortune*. It is not sufficient to see things from far, you must go as close as you can. That is the reason why so many tales begin with a gesture such as knocking at a door or opening a window which expresses a desire to go further, to penetrate more deeply:

'I believe my shadow is the only living thing to be seen over there,' said the learned man. 'How clearly it stands out among the flowers! The door is standing half-open – what a chance for the shadow to pop inside, have a look round and then come and tell me what it has seen! Now then! Make yourself useful! ... Kindly step inside!'[5]

To enter is to try to reach what is most hidden in all things and all beings, to get to know them so intimately that one becomes almost a part of them – an extraordinary journey achieved by a character in *The Goloshes of Fortune* without leaving his seat at the theatre. He is suddenly seized by the desire to enter the hearts of the other spectators:

Now, take all those ladies and gentlemen over there in the front row: if only I could see right inside them – what a revelation it would be – like looking in a shop. My! How my eyes would go shopping! This lady here I should be sure to find running a large dressmaker's ... from one or two might be heard, 'Walk in, sir, do walk in!' Yes, I wish I could walk in and trip through their hearts like a nice, kind thought.

5. *The Shadow.*

Things and people, however ordinary and humble they are, have a secret which has nothing to do with their outward appearance, but which beckons and calls to us, and this gives them a kind of vibration which attracts the viewer's attention. The viewer is the child, discovering his familiar surroundings, looking and *perceiving*, not conditioned by moral and social conventions, but in terms of the emotional relationships he spontaneously creates around him. In this respect some of the games Andersen's children play are very revealing, as when they make use of a specific object without resorting to fancy or to notions picked up in books:

Poor little Elise stood ... playing with a green leaf, for she had no other plaything. She pricked a hole in the leaf and peeped through it at the sun ... [6]

The windows were often quite frozen over, and then they heated pennies on the stove, held the warm copper against the frozen pane, and thus made a little round peep-hole through which they could see each other ... [7]

This closeness of observation, this appreciation of the object from a child's-eye view is the second step towards the conquest of reality. For Hans Andersen what the world around him had to offer was not a store of conventional ideas: living people or inanimate objects affect us, certainly, in terms of the past, but this past is not so much 'history' as the story of each particular person or thing. Hans Andersen's memories are always of a particular kind: they are not primarily concerned with historical or legendary events. Unlike the Scandinavian story-teller Selma Lagerlof, whose inspiration is entirely derived from the legends of her native land, Hans Andersen does not set out to evoke an image of Denmark – except in one or two stories, and these are not his best works. In facts, even if the tales are set in a specific place and describe traditional objects, actions and

6. *The Wild Swans.*
7. *The Snow Queen.*

customs in detail, this is never done to provide local colour. The places – countryside or town – and their inhabitants are described for their own sake – nothing more. Hans Andersen was undoubtedly a national writer, but not a folklorist. He had no particular veneration for the past – in fact he sometimes made fun of historical yearnings and staunchly supported the present day. In *The Goloshes of Fortune*, the councillor's heart 'was full of thankfulness for the happy reality of our own time' when he realized that he had awakened from his medieval nightmare. Memories are everywhere because to be is to have been, and everything in the world – living creatures and inanimate objects – remembers. Creatures and things represent nothing but themselves, however, and the past survives in the present so that a man can relive his childhood experiences whenever he pleases; all he has to do is be on the alert for signs. When a young man finds his tin soldier in the sand he does not recognize it, but he recalls a fragment of his past and for a moment the child he was lives again in him (*The Old House*). Past and present merge in each of us and time is continuous.

Hans Andersen was convinced that childhood never ends. It is not a specific experience in which the human being is confined for a given time, more or less in limbo until he finally starts to live. There was no such break for Hans Andersen between one state and the other; he rejected the need for initiation rites, and saw childhood, forever present and vigorous, continuing to develop for the whole of life. As winter contains all the seeds and the promise of spring, memory preserves childhood intact in the grown man. Thus, in *The Snow Queen* – the parable of Andersen's dearest beliefs – Kay and Gerda, hand in hand, after a long winter find the rose-trees blossoming on the roof in front of the window and their little stools side by side, just as before; the only thing that has changed, in fact, is themselves: they are both grown up; 'There they sat, the two of them, grown up and yet children – children at heart. And it was summer-time, warm, delicious summertime' and the Grandmother was reading these words: 'Except ye become as little children, ye shall not enter into the Kingdom of Heaven . . . '

To be aware of the continuity of time, one must be on the look-out for certain signs. There are favourable moments and also certain messages and unexpected messengers which must be perceived. Space is peopled with organisms, invisible and unimaginable to those who will not see, but they are there, connecting creatures to creation so that the infinity of existence may be perceived. There is the angel – who has nothing in common with the angels of the 'baby Jesus' cult of Christian mythology – and the elves, and the 'daughters of the air', and those particles of light commonly known as sparks; there are, also, other less perceptible messengers: 'And more delicate even than the flame, quite invisible to the human eye, there hovered tiny beings, just as many as there had been blossoms on the flax . . . But the little invisible beings each of them said: "No, no, the song is never over. That is what is so lovely about the whole thing. I know this and that's luckiest of them all".'[8]

These mediating beings are therefore related to the elements air and fire . . . The little mermaid, prisoner of an earthly love, physically and spiritually tortured, regains her free-dom and plenitude of being, not by returning to the sea, but by dissolving into air and rising to the sun, because air and fire are the elements of combustion, which ensures life – and the continuity of life.

In spite of this, people die a great deal in Hans Andersen's fairy tales. His partiality for the macabre is as notorious as his unhappy endings which are so traumatic for small child-ren. His characters die, and often more than once in the same tale. For instance the flax undergoes the pangs of death for the first time when it turns from plant into linen; then

8. *The Flax.*

again when it is made into paper; and lastly when, as a bit of wastepaper, it is thrown into the fire. If death is an end, can this really be death? Not that we find in Hans Andersen's tales any consoling notions of an after-life. No, it is death itself which is seen as a renewal. He forces the reader to ask himself whether death is, in fact, irreversible and final; to wonder how it occurs and what visions accompany it. At the moment of death, the two basic elements air and fire – those life-giving principles which form the very texture of Hans Andersen's thought – are once again present; death comes like a revelation, a sudden flash, an ascent towards the light. This is the symbol contained in the story of *The Little Match-Seller* for whom death is the place where 'it became brighter than broad daylight'. But other characters, too, experience this splendour at the moment of vanishing: the Tin Soldier, melting in the fire with his love, the Dancer:

... when the maid cleaned out the ashes next morning, she found him in the shape of a little tin heart; but all that was left of the dancer was her spangle, and that was burnt black as coal.

The little mermaid 'had no feeling of death. She saw the bright sun ... ' Death is sometimes not even mentioned because it has become synonymous with this luminosity, as in *The Snow Queen*: 'Grannie was sitting there in God's clear sunshine'. This is not rhetoric. The image represents a deeply felt, definite idea. For Hans Andersen physical death is this combustion which ensures the continuity of the species and the permanence of life. Through death the living become light and merge into the universe:

All the paper lay in a bundle on the fire and went flaring up! 'Ooh!' it sighed, and the next moment it was a sheet of flame. It blazed higher into the air than ever the flax had been able to lift its little blue flower ... 'Now I'm going right up into the sun' was the cry from the flame.[9]

9. *The Flax*.

This cannot be seen as an orthodox adherence to the Christian faith in the immortality of the soul and in a life to come. It is rather – and quite simply – a negation of physical death: the Phoenix rising from its ashes, the bird of folk poetry whose voice 'cannot die' and the flaming paper says: 'the song is never over. That is what is so lovely about the whole thing!' For, in fact, nothing dies, not even what seems most vulnerable and transitory – childhood. There are not two distinct worlds, one for grown-ups and one for children, just as life and death are not distinct; there is only a perpetual renewal. Hans Andersen, the poet of continuity and fusion, was the meeting-place of two worlds: in him childhood and manhood merged.

5. *Through the Looking Glass*

The most enduring and the liveliest ingredients in children's literature derive their substance from folklore; all the heroes, even those in Andersen's tales, retain certain characteristics of the folk hero – they are children lost in a wood, outcast younger brothers, beauties in distress. Folk themes always appear to form the basis or frame for children's stories, even if at times such themes are given an unexpected twist or turn, if, for instance, the princess does not marry the prince or the ogre devours Tom Thumb.

In Britain, however, this rule does not always apply, and two of the greatest British children's writers have no immediate connection with folklore: it inspired neither Lewis Carroll nor Edward Lear. The wonderland of this literature has a distinctive character of its own that is deliberately non-realistic. Here, instead of sublimating reality or translating it into symbols, it is completely distorted, an altogether different world emerges from which all the familiar landmarks have been removed, a world of pure fantasy. Yet the liveliness, buffoonery and exaggerations which characterize these stories – though they obviously have no links with folklore – can readily be traced to certain traditional forms such as counting games or nursery rhymes. These jingles – whose origin is often indistinct – collective, spontaneous creations orally transmitted and ritualistically associated with children's games, are to be found in all countries. In England, however, they are not only more popular than elsewhere, they are also more varied and arresting and are not restricted to a mere concatenation of sound, or to a dance rhythm; in the nursery rhyme, the old assonance of freely assembled words conjures up unexpected characters and images. First collected by Newbery, these rhymes have been children's classics ever since, and Old Mother Hubbard, Little Miss Muffet with her spider, Little Jack Horner, the greedy, thieving Knave of Hearts, the Fine Lady on her White Horse and the pugnacious twins, Tweedledum and Tweedledee, have been portrayed by several famous illustrators (Kate Greenaway, Leslie Brooke, Randolph Caldecott etc). They are not only familiar to every English child, but they have also inspired many a writer and poet, and Lewis Carroll, for one, was greatly indebted to them.

The first notable contribution to English children's literature, however, was a very different and specific interpretation of reality – the caricature – Edward Lear's *Book of Nonsense*. The origins of nonsense are as ancient as those of the nursery rhyme, and it is already present in Shakespeare in the form of word-play. Most of Edward Lear's nonsense is in the form of limericks, a five-line verse with a regular rhyme scheme. The first anonymous limericks were printed in anthologies of edifying verse for children. Lear might well have read the following (or a similar one) in *The History of the Sixteen Wonderful Old Women* (1821).

> There was an old lady of Leeds
> Who spent all her time in good deeds;
> She worked for the poor
> Till her fingers were sore
> This pious old lady of Leeds.

He was to write more than two thousand limericks on this

model, giving free rein to his absurd, unpredictable imagination. With Lear, freedom made its appearance in children's literature, thus remedying a sad omission. His whimsical and rather provocative rhymes, plus twenty-odd longer poems, two or three short stories and a *Nonsense Alphabet* were published between 1846 and 1888 and constitute the bulk of Lear's output. His *Book of Nonsense* openly opposes didacticism and boring explanations; it has the candour and vivacity of the best nursery rhymes and an inexhaustible fund of inventiveness that evidently enjoys its own cleverness. Lear himself defined them as 'stuff',

> How pleasant to know Mr Lear
> Who has written such volumes of stuff . . .

and this description cannot be bettered. The rhyme and rhythm bring forth characters, situations and events. These characters are ugly, contorted puppets, cruel but lively and irresistibly funny: they might well be the forebears of those rubber and plastic horrors which are so popular with American children today, but they are also reminiscent of the Marx brothers' creations or of Maurice Sendak's illustrations in *Where the Wild Things Are*. Edward Lear not only describes his characters, he shows us them: he was a professional draughtsman and each of his creations is drawn with a single, relentless stroke of the pen. The mechanical, ritualistic nature of the book casts a spell over the reader and conjures up a completely distorted world which is, nonetheless, perfectly organized and absolutely inevitable; a world where things are what they are because words make them so; where the Dong wears a luminous nose in order to find his Jumbly Girl in the dark – for the Dong only acquires his identity when he becomes 'The Dong with the Luminous Nose'; once the words have been pronounced one can no more escape from the spell than one can escape from a dream.

His absurd inventions are the result of odd fusions of words combined in a mysterious alchemy to produce new compounds, things unheard of. Everybody knows that, for an alchemical operation to be successful, it must be performed with a prescribed ritual and in utter secrecy; it requires ritual knowledge and complete seclusion. And what, indeed, could be more secluded, more isolated from the outside world than the existence of a Victorian child? Paul Hazard[1] suggests that nobody could be happier than an Eton or a Rugby schoolboy of that period; it might be more to the point to say that nobody has ever been more cut off from the world outside and more protected from everyday contingencies. From his earliest childhood, the Victorian child dwelt in a special world where he was alone and where he was king. Adult society had contrived for him two completely artificial kingdoms, the nursery and the public school: he reigned in them, and never stepped outside. Deprived of all external contact, he settled down to a rhythm of his own which escaped the stupid, brutal authority of grown-ups. At school, as in the nursery, he created a whole system of values, a complex hierarchy, that excluded adult interference. This system was based on a master-slave relationship which, in the public school, became what is known as 'fagging'. The 'fag' was a boy from a junior form who acted as confidant, slave and generally as whipping boy for the senior. The relationships which ensued were exempt from adult control and had nothing in common with what, on the continent, would be called friendship or comradeship, but encouraged and rationalized sado-masochistic tendencies in everyday life and were featured in many books of the period also. In spite of the attacks to which it was subjected, even in children's books, it survived for many years, a fact which is borne out by those classics of children's literature, English school

1. op. cit.

stories, from the sublime idealism of the first to be published, *Tom Brown's Schooldays* (1857) by Thomas Hughes, to its ideological not to say literary equivalent, *Stalky & Co.* by Rudyard Kipling, which depicts the vigour and energy of boys happily transforming their artificial environment into a stage setting for their light-hearted but epic battles; from the reforming sentimentality of F. W. Farrar's *Eric or Little by Little* to the liberating violence of Lindsay Anderson's film *If*. For obvious reasons, however, some contact had to be maintained with the adult world: for this, there were different types of intermediary; at school, the prefect armed with his birch rod who was entitled to cane his fellow pupils; at home, servants, particularly the nurse or governess. The servants provided material comfort so that the children were not obliged to come into direct contact with the providers of this comfort, in other words, their parents; they were, at the same time, the children's accomplices, pretending to ignore what took place in the nursery.

The special circumstances in which British children grew up favoured the notion of a separate world, completely self-contained, and where strange, improbable or even impossible things might happen. In the nursery, the dormitory or the classroom, once the door was shut, children were free to perform all kinds of mysterious rituals and to conjure up wonders and monsters in their game. Adults were excluded from this world and knew nothing of what went on. Only a children's writer or a poet could discover these mysteries and that is what Lewis Carroll managed to do. With Dean Liddell's three little girls in a boat on the river, he wiled away a long summer afternoon telling them the story of *Alice's Adventures in Wonderland* (1865). Looking at Alice Liddell's angelic little face, it is difficult to see how she could have inspired such an ambivalent tale. But then, the little girls Carroll was wont to photograph all had the innocent faces and wide trusting eyes that distinguish those

other little innocents in *The Turn of the Screw* by Henry
James. *The Turn of the Screw* (1898) was intended to be a
study of evil: it is a descent into hell, the confrontation of
complete innocence with total perversion. Here, the basic
theme of the relationship between children and servants is
reversed and its black side shown. It is not the little master
and mistress who draw the servants into their guileless
games of make-believe but, rather, the servants who are in
complete control and lead the children to the frontiers of
sin and evil. The servants' task was the easier because,
behind the charming faces and the limpid gaze, lurks that
unknown region, the unconscious. Thus a child's soul –
that mixture of sunlight and shadow – is an easy prey for
diabolical influences. Childhood is capable of everything,
even of raising ghosts. But *The Turn of the Screw* is the ultimate in exploration of a child's psyche, and not a book for
children.

Alice is, however, essentially a children's book. It is
probably one of the first books for children to have been
made up for and with a child, with no other object than to
entertain and to appeal directly to the imagination. It is also
one of the first literary explorations – at least where children's literature is concerned – of that fundamental human
feeling, anxiety. The anxiety of *Alice in Wonderland* is
typically that of a child: it pervades the book from the very
first pages, investing every improbable encounter and each
hilarious adventure. We find a child's anxiety at not growing
up fast enough, perhaps never growing up, allied to a refusal
to grow up; the traumatic experience of seeing one's own
body in strange, incomprehensible metamorphoses that
often seem shameful or even monstrous. A child frequently
finds his body a source of embarrassment which, at certain
stages in his development, can become almost painfully
acute and these incommunicable sensations of bewilderment
and disorientation – often translated into compensatory

attitudes of braggadocio – have nowhere been better expressed than in Alice's adventures. Carroll also explores minutely all the degrees of inhibition a child can feel in the presence of adults. Alice is tongue-tied and incapable of finding answers to the questions that are put to her; she is stupefied by the clamour of incomprehensible conversations and she cannot make herself heard – or when she does, her words are distorted or dismissed in summary fashion. The March Hare's tea-party is perhaps the best illustration of the intractability and inadequacy of language as experienced by a child in adult company but there are examples in every chapter of both the *Alice* books. The child's loneliness and inability to merge with the adult world give him a distorted vision of reality. It is not so much that words do not mean anything: on the contrary, their significance is preserved too literally – so that language becomes impenetrable. When words are taken literally we are the prisoners of language and of the insuperable barriers of its logic. In the dialogue between Alice and the White Queen where, because yesterday, today and tomorrow signify precisely yesterday, today and tomorrow, they can never be experienced:

'I'm sure I'll take you with pleasure!' the Queen said. 'Two pence a week and jam every other day.'

Alice couldn't help laughing, as she said, 'I don't want you to hire *me*, and I don't care for jam.'

'It's very good jam,' said the Queen.

'Well, I don't want any *today* at any rate.'

'You couldn't have it if you *did* want it,' the Queen said. 'The rule is, jam tomorrow and jam yesterday – but never jam *today*.'

'It *must* come sometimes to "jam today".' Alice objected.

'No, it can't,' said the Queen. 'It's jam every *other* day; today isn't any *other* day, you know.'

'I don't understand you,' said Alice. 'It's dreadfully confusing!'[2]

But although words are forever fixed in their literal

2. *Alice Through the Looking Glass.*

meanings, objects and people keep on turning into something else. The visible world is blurred and evasive, or undergoes sudden preposterous mutations: babies become pigs and old women sheep, the Cheshire Cat vanishes leaving behind only its grin and at the end Alice finds herself in a land inhabited by monsters. These monsters are either the denizens of the nursery-rhyme world like the Knave of Hearts, Tweedledum and Tweedledee, Humpty Dumpty etc., or they are the products of everyday sayings and are absurd because they are the logical interpretations of the words. The British do say 'as mad as a hatter' and the mock turtle is drawn as a turtle with a calf's head because there is a soup made from a calf's head called 'mock turtle soup'.

Words create creatures and objects and permit weird associations; words also create their own causality: because the snark was a boojum the baker's death was inevitable – whence the poem . . . and Lewis Carroll himself gives us the recipe.

> For first you write a sentence,
> And then you chop it small;
> Then mix the bits, and sort them out
> Just as they chance to fall:
> The order of the phrases makes
> No difference at all.3

Lewis Carroll's creations are very much alive; some, like the caterpillar or the white rabbit, have haunting personalities. Others, like the mock turtle, owe their oddity to a linguistic peculiarity and thus strike the English-speaking

3. *Poeta fit non nascitur*. This has been restated almost *verbatim* in *Pour faire un poème Dadaiste* by Tristan Tzara (1920): 'Take a newspaper – take a pair of scissors – choose an article in the paper of the right length for your poem – cut it out then carefully cut out each word and put them in a bag – shake before emptying contents onto a table – copy conscientiously – your poem will be true to type – and you will thus have become a very original poet gifted with an adorable sensitivity though misunderstood by the mob.'

child as old acquaintances, more comic than disturbing, but for the foreign reader, they are totally irrational and therefore the more disturbing.

Indeed the first French translators realized this and tried to make some of the Alice poems – the lively parodies of contemporary poems – into comic travesties of La Fontaine *Fables*; however, this laid too much stress on a single aspect of the book at the expense of its many others, but it may serve as an example of the fact that *Alice's Adventures in Wonderland* is really a national book with its roots firmly embedded in the English childhood lore.

Lewis Carroll did not fully realize the forces he had un-leashed. After his two masterpieces *Alice's Adventures in Wonderland* and *Alice through the Looking Glass* and some nonsense poems, he decided to write a book for good child-ren: *Sylvie and Bruno* was a patchy, inconsistent book, some-times brilliant in its manically repetitive style, but, on balance, can only be considered a failure.[4] Alice remains unique, but she had blazed the trail.

Children and childhood had become enigmas. Stories were no longer based on observations of the visible world or on the consciousness of being and existing as in Hans Ander-sen, they were now about the child psyche. From Carroll to the present day, children's writers have tried to unravel its secrets. In their attempts to penetrate the mysteries of the nursery they created the persona of the 'enfant terrible'. For Jean Cocteau, the children's games in the claustrophobic atmosphere of 'the room' where the general untidiness represents the negation of all discipline – the hoarding of treasure, the innocent promiscuity, the quarrels and especially the systematic practice of compensatory day-dreams or what they called 'going away' – all these games played with total concentration and taken to extreme limits, could lead only to disaster. The children's room is the stage

4. Cf. Jean Gattegno's thesis: *Lewis Carroll*, José Corti, Paris, 1970.

where four wild creatures perform a passionate dance of love and death like the characters from classical tragedy. In Cocteau, children's writer and the writer about children meet. It is a moot point whether one should present an adolescent with such a picture of himself but it is hard to say exactly what should or should not be admissible as children's literature.

The frontier depends, in fact, on the degree of pessimism with which the writer looks at the world. A capacity for silence, for dissimulation, born of day-dreaming or devilment, capriciousness and other manifestations of childish perversity can be very differently interpreted; just as *A Midsummer Night's Dream* can be seen as fairy tale or horrific nightmare.

Le Grand Meaulnes' way leads him through the forest to the Park, the castle and the enchantment of the 'strange ball', in *The Explorers of the Dawn* by Mazo de la Roche, the children's association with the maid, the butcher's boy and the tramps turns the dismal house ruled by a strict governess into a pleasure-ground full of untold surprises and in Henri Bosco's Provençal landscapes, superstitions, in the eyes of a child, become magic spells.

Diametrically opposed to these idyllic visions are the portraits of children in *A High Wind in Jamaica* by Richard Hughes or in *Lord of the Flies* by William Golding, where children have to live their own nightmares. These stories are, in fact, attempts to retrieve the past – excursions into memory where the reality of childhood is seen objectively. Even in the most ruthless of these novels there is a basic element of nostalgia: these are adult reminiscences, grown-up endeavours to solve the mysteries of a lost childhood. The adult is present all the time, he cannot leave the children alone so that when the reader has finished, say, *The Turn of the Screw* (undoubtedly the most successful and the most disturbing work of this kind) he does not know where

3

objectivity ends and subjectivity begins. Is the supernatural evoked by the children or is it the outcome of an adult interpretation of their inner lives? He is left wondering whether what he has read is a poetic yet faithful representation of the dark powers of childhood or the clinical analysis of a morbid adult imagination.

In other books, intuition takes over from memory and the narrator abstains from intervening. He is entirely free from preconceived theories about childhood – or at least he tries to forget them. We find ourselves in the presence of children who talk and play together just as if nobody were observing them. They discuss their identity and their tastes – which happen to be precisely those of their readers:

'I'm beastly bored,' said Robert.

'Let's talk about the Psammead,' said Anthea who generally tried to give the conversation a cheerful turn.

'What's the good of *talking*?' said Cyril. 'What I want is for something to happen ... '

Jane finished the last of her home lessons and shut the book with a bang.

'We've got the pleasures of memory,' said she ...

'I don't want to think about the pleasures of memory,' said Cyril; 'I want some more things to happen.'

'We're much luckier than anyone else as it is,' said Jane. 'Why, no one else ever found a Psammead. We ought to be grateful.'

'Why shouldn't we *go on* being, though?' Cyril asked – 'lucky, I mean; not grateful. Why's it all got to stop?'

'Perhaps something will happen,' said Anthea, comfortably. 'Do you know, sometimes I think we are the sort of people that things *do* happen to.'5

A writer who knows which are the children 'that things *do* happen to' and how to surprise them at their games without being observed, and who has, besides, the gift of taking children for granted, has the makings of a good

5. E. Nesbit, *The Phoenix and the Carpet*.

children's writer. At the head of this class are the English, but they are not the only ones with this gift. For a literature of make-believe to be successful it must be restricted to the world of childhood, a closed system where everything suits its dimensions and conventions. Its time is 'now', an eternal present where clocks tick to the rhythm of the story, as in certain classics of the genre such as *The Cuckoo-Clock* by Mrs Molesworth, *Tom's Midnight Garden* by Philippa Pearce and some of E. Nesbit's books, notably *The House of Arden*. This sort of book is also static in terms of space; the child-heroes do, of course, leave their rooms but their explorations are limited to their own world and lead nowhere; once the adventure is over they go back to the nursery again.*
Instead of travelling from one point to another, however rambling the journey, their pilgrimage describes a circle – a pre-eminently magic figure – which Kipling declared to be the only sign with any power over the supernatural world.[6] The children are whisked away in a maelstrom of magic that does not influence their lives: such adventures have nothing to do with experience and leave the adventurers as childish afterwards as they were before, no wiser and not a day older. To enliven and animate the story the author can only multiply the number of protagonists: baby brothers or sisters join the group, or a new arrival in the neighbourhood who also happens to possess 'the gift'. But this is, in fact, nothing but a mirror effect: each character resembles the others, and they are all equally stereotyped, so that there can never be any conflict; they share the same secrets and are subject to the same enchantments at identical times.

An example of this type of hero carried to an extreme is

* Editor's note: There are exceptions to this: E. Nesbit's *Harding's Luck*, the sequel to *The House of Arden*, shows the new sense of identity in the hero, who finally sacrifices his chance of living a privileged life in this century for the sake of a family honour about which he didn't know at the beginning of the book.

6. *Puck of Pook's Hill.*

Peter Pan who haunts the Serpentine and Kensington Gardens, and especially the island – an appropriately enclosed, circular spot where according to Barrie, all the babies who are about to be born disport themselves freely with the water-birds until their time has come. For Peter Pan the time has come and gone: the clock has stopped and he will always remain a baby, spending his life between the island and Kensington Gardens where those children who *will* grow up play. Like all stories of make-believe – but more so than most – the story of Peter Pan symbolizes the child's reluctance to be absorbed into adult life, his fear of reality which motivates his flight and leads to the parallel, upside-down world on the other side . . . through the looking glass and beyond consciousness. Such a flight, however, is far from easy: it is not enough to be a child for looking-glass land to become immediately accessible and the rejection of reality does not automatically provide free entry. Children do not, as a rule, cross its frontiers alone, they require a sponsor and a guide, and the creation of this guide is a good measure of a writer's inventive powers. The easiest, most direct and reassuring guide is probably the toy. One of the first stories of a doll's house becoming large enough for children to enter and in which they can move about with greater comfort and ease than in the confusions of reality comes, naturally enough, from Germany – the country (with Italy) where the making of dolls, toys and puppets has always been a speciality. *The Nut-cracker* is probably the only one of E. T. A. Hoffman's tales which appeals to children; it is also one of the most accomplished of those about a land of toys. In *Winnie-the-Pooh* by A. A. Milne, another well-known book, of the same sort, characters are less disturbing than those of *The Nut-cracker*; they are the very young child's toys, cuddly, mischievous, clumsy animals who are funny and endearing. In *Winnie-the-Pooh* the child can enjoy the pleasure of feeling superior at the same

time as he hugs himself in a sort of self-pity. Other charming books of this kind worth mentioning are Monteiro
Lobato's Brazilian stories which humorously place a grandmother, an old cook and an ear of maize on the same level
of communication. Rumer Godden's stories sound a more
mysterious note and are disquieting in the minuteness of
their descriptions. They are alive with a sense of waiting
(rarely fulfilled) – of dolls waiting for someone to play with
them. Theirs is a rarefied world dealing only in the purest
emotions of sadness or joy.*

Such stories are always on the verge of becoming stilted
and therefore stories about entirely make-believe people are
more readily acceptable. It is of course, quite usual for
children at some stage to invent a beloved imaginary companion – the younger brother or sister or the pet animal of
which they have been deprived – and it is this trait which is
here exploited. In some cases the make-believe is a whole
kingdom which makes up for the short-comings of real life
while remaining entirely independent of it. Since the publication of the Brontë's notebooks their imaginary kingdom
of Angria is always quoted as a typical example of such a
compensatory world whose spell, in this case, was not
broken even by growing up.

Children's writers are often stimulated by the challenge
of an imaginary world which will be more real than reality.
Lucy Boston in the *Green Knowe* series has succeeded remarkably well in this task, thanks to an extreme delicacy of touch
and a rare circumspection. On the other hand, Philippa
Pearce's books are more direct and consequently more
accessible to children, though her first novel, *Tom's Midnight
Garden* is perhaps a little too complacent, not withstanding its

---

* Editor's note: See also *The Tapestry Room* by Mrs Molesworth and
another slightly disturbing tale by the same author, *The Reel Fairies*, in which
the contents of her mother's workbox, the silk and cotton reels, come to
life and treat little Louisa with less kindness than she might have expected.

real charm. Everybody knows that most old country houses are haunted without having to read Lucy Boston or Philippa Pearce, and just because Miss Pearce's ghosts are so convincing one might have feared that she would systematically exploit this theme, turning her real gifts into a mere gimmick. However, her second book *A Dog so Small* allayed such fears. It is a particularly successful attempt at depicting a child's imaginary relationship with an invisible being. Here the reality of the make-believe dog becomes more and more convincing – though the dog remains invisible throughout. And the end, when the spell is broken and everyday life obtrudes, is not contrived and leaves the reader entirely satisfied – a rare achievement in this sort of book, where the difficulty consists in the readjustment to reality, in the manner of presenting the re-entry into existence. Some writers try to avoid this pitfall by turning their stories into fables which conclude with a warning against the dangers of make-believe. Among these we find Antonia Forest's strange novel, *Peter's Room*, a book which is, unfortunately, too allusive to be appreciated by any but the upper-class English child. It describes the ill-fated attempt by a group of children to relive the young Brontë's experience. Another example is *Chwambranie* by the excellent Soviet writer Leo Cassil, where the lesson is given with humour and in such a manner as to appeal to children of every country and class.

Writers who give free rein to their imagination yet simultaneously refuse to be taken in by their own creations and even, at times, denounce them, appeal by the very ambiguity of their attitude to older children of the pre-adolescent age-group – children, in fact, who have usually ceased to believe in fairies but still like the idea. When books are written with younger readers in mind their authors can afford to be less cautious. The children they are addressing want something more than a common or garden toy, they aren't satisfied with talking to themselves, but need an imaginary companion who will answer back. The English writer, E. Nesbit, excelled – after Lewis Carroll – in the art of creating strange and entirely credible creatures such as the psammead who puffed himself out to grant wishes, the mouldiwarp who ruled over white objects only, and the vain phoenix. The children in these stories are in complete possession of the 'gift'. They move as naturally from their play-room into the land of make-believe as they eat their porridge and go for walks in the Park. To Nesbit's imaginative novels (the *Five Children* series, *The House of Arden*, and *The Enchanted Castle*), can be added Pamela Travers's story of the fairy nursemaid *Mary Poppins*. Miss Travers's inventions are both ingenious and ingenuous – for instance the star-polishing incident or the laughing-gas scene – and Mary Poppins herself is all the more convincing as a modern witch in that her supernatural powers are concealed under a prim and puritanical exterior. Yet there is, in *Mary Poppins*, a certain indulgence towards magic, and the feeling that the author tends to make the children's wishes conform to a conventional, poeticized notion of what an adult hopes a child should want, rather than to the trivial or even gross wishes a child would be more likely to formulate. Nesbit's young heroes on the other hand, have the lively insolence of normal children whose wishes are simple and realistic: they ask for wings to fly, to be more beautiful than the day or to get rid of a tiresome baby brother . . . and the author's robust imagination always provides a magic solution which sparks off a series of ludicrous catastrophes.

Nesbit is undoubtedly a better psychologist than Pamela Travers and to some extent a more spontaneous and more genuine writer. Her integrity forbids her to tamper with the logical sequence of her stories; ill-conceived games topple over into nightmare; childish jokes take on something of tragedy, as in her most ambitious books, *Harding's Luck* and *The Enchanted Castle*. Why, therefore, have her books never 'taken' abroad while a trivial story like *Mary Poppins* is immensely popular? Probably, as with the Comtesse de Ségur who is unknown outside France, the books are too highly flavoured and will not export. E. Nesbit's writing, however, does have many faults: her language and outlook are dated and so are the middle-class Edwardian family backgrounds she describes, whereas Miss Travers writes lucidly and simply without any superfluity and sets her story squarely in the timeless but perennial sphere of the fairy tale.

To these 'other worlds' must be added C. S. Lewis's *Narnia*. Lewis's books are deservedly popular but his imagination tends to run dry and has to resort to German folklore and ancient mythologies to people Narnia with dwarfs and fauns; nevertheless this is done with sufficient spontaneity and assurance to make them unexpected and convincing. Some may prefer Frank Baum's *The Wizard of Oz* to this rather derivative cycle. Its magic is less well integrated into the stories and not so charged with cultural and moral overtones, but the 'land of Oz', despite the author's refreshingly simple style, remains only a decorative backcloth. The book deserves its popularity but Carl Sandburg's *Rootabaga Stories* are more vigorous. His mastery of language, free imagination and pleasant sense of humour enable this great American poet to communicate with children on equal terms.

This might also be the place to mention Aymé's *Contes du chat perché*. The heroines, Delphine and Marinette, certainly inhabit a world of their own, but, unlike the world of English children's literature, theirs is not arbitrary, for it is against the grown-ups that they join forces with the farm animals who reveal their legendary gifts to the two little girls. Such an attitude of self-defence on the part of children is almost unheard of in England where the adult world is not so opposed to the child's and where, apart from the servants – whose function has already been discussed – there exists a peculiar species of adult intermediary – what Barrie called 'betwixt-betweens' – the English eccentric. Children always have the chance of getting to know an absent-minded professor or an elderly unmarried lady whose wits are slightly astray, in whom they will find a friend. These eccentrics have the unusual gift of remaining individuals while still remembering how to play as a child plays. This peculiarity is completely unfamiliar to the adults in Marcel Aymé's stories, who have practically no individual existence. They are, in fact, no more than their social function: the parents, the schoolmaster, the schoolmistress or the mayor. And as it is impossible to hold a conversation with a name, Delphine and Marinette talk to the animals on the farm. However, in the bright, clear, Île-de-France light magic does not easily thrive and the conversations which ensue are not entirely credible. The *Contes du chat perché* contribute a new dimension to the literature of make-believe, a dimension that English books for children often ignore, that of irony.*

Sometimes the frontiers of reality collapse altogether. The hero himself is a fantastic being – a 'betwixt-between'. The first of such characters to appear in children's literature was probably Pinocchio, but Pinocchio is not a denizen from another planet. Basically, he is no different from a child; his unusual appearance – derived, like that of his cousin Nils Holgersson, from national folklore, the puppet for Pinocchio, the troll for Nils – has a definite cause: both Pinocchio and Nils are children in disgrace and their outward appearance is a form of punishment, accidental and transitory, rather than an essential part of their nature.

* Editor's note: One outstanding example of irony in a recent children's book is *Speaking Terms* by Mary Exton in which children and animals find that they can communicate in language. This book is also an interesting exception to most animal stories written for children in that its main characteristic is humour and irony without sentiment.

3*

On the other hand the tales of Otfried Preussler – who tries to create his own Valhalla – do not portray human beings of any kind. Similarly *Vevi*, the weird root-child of Erika Lillig's story, leads an entirely marginal existence. There seems to be one distinctive feature which all these imaginary creatures have in common and that is their diminutive size. This secluded world usually retains that characteristic of childhood and it is not surprising that Lilliput appeals more to the imagination than Brobdingnag – a fact which Winterfeld proves very cleverly in his story *Télégramme de Lilliput* (if, indeed, any proof were required). Trolls are particular favourites with children, and among the more successful books that feature these strange beings are J. R. R. Tolkien's *Hobbit*, Wolson's *Le Royaume des marmousets*, Mary Norton's *The Borrowers* and Tove Jansson's *Moomins*. These last, truly improbable beings come to life in the author's incomparable drawings as well as in her prose. On first opening *Finn Family Moomintroll*, the reader is at a loss as to the true nature of these happy little creatures – they might equally well be children, insects, pixies or mice, but the more distinct such creatures are from nature, the more commonplace their adventures seem to grow. There is a world of difference between these tales and Lewis Carroll's wonderland. Some of them – the *Moomins* or *Wiplala* by Annie Schmidt, do set out to create a feeling of unreality and magic, but others, like *The Borrowers*, contain no such elements and the magic, even when it does exist, is put to the most realistic and trivial of uses; for instance, in the *Moomin* books the characters' main preoccupation is not to gain entrance into an enchanted garden but to find Mother Moomin's handbag. The insistence on detail is only enhanced by the microscope size of the protagonists. Perhaps this is the child's true world – not impossible flights of fancy but a search for the miniature in life.

This could explain the relative unpopularity of science fiction for children outside the U.S.A. and the U.S.S.R., and Madeleine l'Engle's books are the best in this field.* On the other hand, the trolls' ambiguity, the fact that they are definitely not human, yet are represented in human situations, satisfies the conflicting childish needs for change and for stability.

The causes for this tendency of imaginative literature to become more realitic are not far to seek. In the first place, the circumstances of children's lives have changed enormously in recent years; even in England the gulf between their world and that of the adult is gradually decreasing. Admittedly English children's literature still indulges in magic and make-believe, but children who are not brought up by nurses in a nursery and for whom public school lore is something they know only by hearsay or from books, find it difficult to appreciate fantasy, so it is not surprising if the books written for them tend more and more to be based on a general family life. To be successful, children's stories must correspond to real experiences: Victorian children experienced mainly isolation and confinement but this is no longer remotely the case with today's children. With the notable exception of Lewis Carroll and some of E. Nesbit's books where the glimpse of mysterious life behind the nursery door is authentic, the deliberate unreality of most of these stories fails to satisfy children's imaginations, while adults find them too contrived. Is it because such stories are too often based on a false or distorted notion of a child's real needs? Just because a child is reluctant to face the world as it is, does not necessarily imply that he rejects it. If he shrinks from direct contact with reality and tries to find a convenient, reassuring mediator to act as buffer

* Editor's note: In the last six years there has been a sudden uprush of science fiction writing for children, i.e. John Christopher, Nicolas Fisk, André Norton and Peter Dickinson.

between himself and it, this is surely not in order to escape from it. Children, on the contrary, are very fond of imitating reality; their games are always real – more real than reality. They play at mundane things like 'shops' or they enact situations they do not entirely comprehend like 'mothers and fathers' or 'war'. They do not oppose reality, rather, they try to grasp it and to adapt adult conceptions to their own mental capacity.

The quality that all these books – and in particular E. Nesbit's – have in common and what guarantees their success is their objectivity. Strange beings appear and strange things happen, but not for the sake of creating a mystery and certainly not to conform to a hypothetical 'poetic world of childhood'. The child is left to unravel the threads and separate the real from the imaginary; nothing is prejudged, the scales are not weighted.

A book like Saint-Exupéry's famous *Le petit prince* is perplexing both for adults and children. It is the prototype of the work on two levels; it is about childhood yet apparently addressed to children. Children are shown as living in a world of their own and are therefore fundamentally different from grown-ups – they can see things the adult is no longer able to perceive. Thus it is the adult who plays at make-believe while the child is really living and dealing with serious matters such as the rose and the stars. The author, with one foot in each world, tries to explain the child to the adult and the child to himself. However, such a clear-cut demarcation between the two worlds is arbitrary, not to say misleading; these are not, in fact, systematically opposed states but complementary ones whose interplay can be perceived by poets. *Le petit prince* is an essentially didactic work in that it is an exposition of Saint-Exupéry's thoughts on the subject of innocence – and is therefore mainly of interest to the Saint-Exupéry fan. However, children are informed in this statement addressed primarily to them, that they inhabit a distant, ideal planet where love is truly love and they cannot fail to be flattered by such a view. But this does not alter the fact that he expresses a rather superficially manichean and pessimistic conception of the world in a not very inspiring symbolism; pure, altruistic reactions are confined to the heavens – or more precisely to the star 'where love is forever' as the song goes.

There is infinitely more subtlety and at the same time more life in Maurice Maeterlinck's *The Bluebird* which also sets out to prove something. Like Hans Andersen, though in a very different vein and in a different poetical convention, Maeterlinck tries to establish a dialogue between the two worlds. *L'Oiseau bleu* achieves the very difficult task of enabling its guileless child-heroes to attain true wisdom quite naturally and without ever sounding categorical or dogmatic; they express themselves almost exclusively in questions. Tyltyl and Mytyl ask questions all the time and everything fills them with wonder. But they are also willing to play at any time, something the melancholy, academic petit Prince never does. As in Hans Andersen's stories, the make-believe is never laboured and is often witty. Even in the presence of bewildering miracles, human beings are still able – though perhaps too rarely willing – to avoid taking themselves too seriously; they can smile at the antics of Cold-in-the-Head when surrounded by the most terrifying Mysteries and appalling Disasters; in the midst of Great Happiness and deep tender Domestic Bliss they know the Pleasure-of-running-bare-foot-in-the-dew and even the Pleasure-of-being-a-Nuisance, because the one thing that matters is to be in touch with reality. What inspires the reader's imagination is the writer's original view of the real world. That is why, whatever their shortcomings, *The Borrowers* and *Moomins* which sing the praise of everyday reality, are among the more successful attempts at children's literature today. One cannot, however, use them as a formula. A good book is not made by inventing a troll family and placing it in absurd or pathetic situations; and though it is among today's books of this kind that some of tomorrow's classics may be found, it is also in this genre that the author runs the greatest risk of writing artificially, with too many words and false poetic sentiment.

6. *Animal Land*

Children tend to clothe the animate world in disturbing or reassuring shapes in order to feel their way in a world of incessantly changing and elusive presences where only emotions and events remain stable. The most common form of transformation is, of course, into animals. There are affinities between animals and imaginary beings such as trolls in Scandinavian stories, or fabulous creatures in *Alice in Wonderland* and puppets and caricature figures. We also have supernatural beasts in folklore, that mythical menagerie generated at the beginning of time – magic horses, animals who can speak, curse or reward – but whose features can still be recognized in some of the characters of modern tales, such as Nesbit's strange 'fairies', the farm animals of the *Contes du chat perché* or Elwyn White's book, *Charlotte's Web*. On this idyllic American farm, children and good animals live side by side, democratically accepting the spider as the personification of superior intelligence. Animals, however, are always ambiguous in such books – 'betwixt-between' – that is, they mediate between the natural and the supernatural world and are animals in name only. In such tales non-human beings – whether mythical or not – exist only in relation to human beings. Their strange, unpredictable behaviour is a consequence of their ambivalence: on the one hand they are earthly beings, sharing man's sufferings and labours, marking out his path in the same way as the rest of nature – elements, plants, minerals – and on the other they are in communication with supernatural powers and thus able to help man to realize his destiny. The world of real animals is another matter altogether. If this world is to be depicted in its true relationship to man, animals can no longer retain their magic powers, they must be allowed to recover their natural dignity, lost in the transition from animal-gods to the homely, smiling figure of Puss-in-Boots; they must be hunted, trapped and used for material, not spiritual, ends. In other words, they must become creatures dominated by man and not on an equal footing with him as in the old folk tales where they repaid human kindness with gifts. Animals will have to be detached from the human world and re-integrated into nature, their true element; they must cease to be a man-made symbol and become wild beasts, and to do this requires an unusual insight, respect and powers of observation; qualities which Rudyard Kipling possessed to a high degree and of which he made good use when he wrote the first book of this kind, *The Jungle Book* in 1894. It is interesting to note that this western writer was imbued with a deep knowledge of India, its scenery and mythology and that India is the country, according to the *Ramayana*, where poetry first emerged, from the tears shed by man over a dove he had killed in flight. Western man, tutored by the civilizations of Ancient Greece and Rome, by Judaism and Christianity, has always ignored nature and never tried to befriend the animal world. As Michelet says:

Notwithstanding its greater gentleness Christianity inherited the Jewish attitude towards nature; the Jews, in their wisdom, dreaded too great an attachment to this sister of mankind, so they were careful to avoid it and disparage it. Christianity preserved this distrust and kept the animal realm at a distance and disparaged it. The symbolic beasts of the Evangelists and the intellectual allegories of the Lamb and the Dove did nothing to reinstate animals. They were not included in the new Blessing;

the littlest and humblest creatures were not to know salvation. The Man-God died for men and not for them. Having no share in salvation they remained outside the pale of Christian law, pagan and unclean and often accused of conniving with the powers of evil. Did not the Christ of the Gospels allow devils to take possession of the swine?[1]

Michelet goes on to recall that the cows and the ass only crept into the Nativity legend because of popular feeling. There is, however, one great Christian poem in praise of man's link with nature and the beasts: a poem which incites mankind to join nature in an act of devotion to the Creator of all things; this is the beautiful 'Canticle of the Creatures' of Saint Francis of Assisi. But in art animals continued to be represented unlovingly and conventionally and were mainly pretexts for intellectual effects. The western fable tradition shows the influence of this attitude, for in these fables animals are simply pretexts enabling the writer to show human predicaments and an excuse for unrestrained censure and satire. Animal fables for children have a long history which starts with *Roman de Renart* and the *Fables* of La Fontaine. It is impossible to attempt to define and analyse it here, but a rough outline may be established in an attempt to penetrate the child-reader's attitude by determining the proportions of anthropomorphism and observation: when, for example, do the animals in a fable act as animals and when do they become men and women, and which of these two interpretations is likely to appeal to the child. If the balance falters[2] and leans too heavily on the side of an exaggerated anthropomorphism the story tends to become trite and we have the dreary, laboured caricature in the manner of Benjamin Rabier or the *Contes de mon père le Jars* by Léonce Bourliaguet with their ridiculous animal

1. Michelet, *Le Peuple*, vol. II, chapter VI, Paris, 1846.
2. A perfect balance is perhaps achieved in Hugh Lofting's *Dr Dolittle* stories.

foremen and animal engineers. The equivalent in the English language would perhaps be the cartoon animals of Walt Disney or even the cats of Louis Wayne at the beginning of this century.

Among the moral fables with animal heroes there are a few outstanding works such as *La famosa invasione degli orsi in Sicilia* by Dino Buzzati for younger children, and *Animal Farm* by George Orwell for the more sophisticated. Both these books depict an animal society based on the same principles as human society – in Buzzati on a simple and pleasantly humanistic moral code; in Orwell on the fundamental data of socialism. These societies aim at nothing less than perfection and they are confronted with all the intrinsically human elements of corruption which impair and distort the best intentions. The question is: Will the animals be better equipped than human beings to defend themselves against self-interest and lust for power? The most remarkable thing about these two books is that the dramatization is never overshadowed by the author's desire to prove a point and that the animals, if they are not perhaps the bears and pigs of our natural history books, are definitely not human beings in disguise as they tend to be in *Roman de Renart*, for instance.

Both Orwell and Buzzati in their different ways make a point of stressing their heroes' peculiar individualities. The story only works because their bears and pigs are recognizably different from human beings and the disasters which befall them arise because they try to step outside their specific animal natures and imitate men. In Buzzati the result is a common-sensical and good-humouredly moralizing tale, but in George Orwell's novel the significance is much more profound.

Buzzati's bears, Orwell's pigs, and their relatives, the fox and the cat in *Pinocchio* – or indeed any of the sharp-tongued, furred or feathered creatures who star in this kind of story –

cannot be said to exist as individuals in their own right, despite the author's intentions. The reader can hardly picture them as animals and only the names subsist as a kind of joke: brave bear, cunning fox, cat-bandit or pig-despot, the type completely submerges the personality – unless of course, illustrations assist the author's task, as in the case of Buzzati's bears. As a rule, the animal hero comes to life only in pictures and illustrators are always partial to animals. One might even go so far as to say that the animal hero needs this added prop in order to exist as a character, although Black Beauty is clearly an exception. Bambi, the roe-buck hero of a charming tale by the Austrian writer Felix Salten, would have been just a shadowy figure like so many others in the genre if the cinema had not stepped in. The cinema has, in fact, created a stereotype of the little deer that is totally synthetic: the deer is no longer a deer but an eternal Bambi.

Some animals have thus achieved a sort of deification thanks to illustrations or films and come to personify their species as mythical heroes in the child's mind. Every rabbit is a Beatrix Potter flopsy bunny and every elephant a Babar. Illustrations also give an additional pleasure; when a child sees an appealing picture of an animal he is often overcome with delight. Small children have an extremely acute sense of touch: they love to handle and stroke soft fluffy objects, and the first thing they do when looking at a picture is to stroke the surface and follow the outlines with their little fingers, thereby gratifying their senses of touch and sight. The elephant's odd shape and the soft cuddly rabbit satisfy their simple but powerful sensual needs and it is precisely to this childish sensuality that animal stories appeal; a sympathetic understanding of the animal is stimulated which focuses initially on the picture: 'how soft', 'how cuddly', 'how sweet'. From this starting-point a truer sympathy can later be stimulated.

The exception to all that has been said about animals only becoming heroes once they have been represented in pictures is Kipling. His marvellous characters live through the written word alone and they are all beasts living wild in their natural environment: Shere-Khan the tiger, Kaa the snake, Baloo the brown bear, Bagheera the panther, Mother Wolf and all the other creatures of the Indian tales, the tales of the Great North or the *Just so Stories*. Human communication with these animals is not contrived or based on a system of gifts or services rendered; it is a simple, organic communion of bodily rhythms – the human heartbeat corresponds equally to that of the animal and both respond to the vibrations of the earth. Kipling speaks of the naked human baby – 'a wise little frog' – and of its brother-cubs in identical terms. The little mahout, perched on the back of the great elephant Kala Nag, feels the painful rhythm of the elephant dance in all the nerves of his body.

> . . . and little Toomai put his hands up to his ears to shut out the sound. But it was all one gigantic jar that ran through him – this stamp of hundreds of heavy feet on the raw earth. Once or twice he could feel Kala Nag and all the others surge forward a few strides, and the thumping would change to the crushing sound of juicy green things being bruised, but in a minute or two the boom of feet on hard earth began again. A tree was creaking and groaning somewhere near him. He put out his arm and felt the bark, but Kala Nag moved forward still tramping, and he could not tell where he was in the clearing. There was no sound from the elephants, except once, when two or three little calves squeaked together. Then he heard a thump and a shuffle, and the booming went on. It must have lasted fully two hours and Little Toomai ached in every nerve.[3]

When the child experiences something which is alien to the animals, the break is final and complete:

3. 'Toomai of the Elephants', in *The Jungle Books*.

'What is it? What is it?' he said. 'I do not wish to leave the jungle, and I do not know what this is. Am I dying, Bagheera?'

'No, Little Brother. Those are only tears such as men use,' said Bagheera. 'Now I know thou art a man, and a man's cub no longer. The Jungle is shut indeed to thee henceforward. Let them fall, Mowgli. They are only tears.'[4]

Kipling's great contribution to books about animals was this total, physical awareness of their pulsating life and an acceptance and understanding of their nature, and this was coincidental with a new departure in education. Intellectual development alone was no longer paramount; total education should also take account of a child's physical and sensual capabilities. Physical fitness and an ability to make use of all five senses were considered as important in forming his personality as were a knowledge of spelling and arithmetic. These basic principles of the 'New Education' were variously interpreted and led to the establishment of such movements as the Boy Scouts for whom *The Jungle Books* were for many years a sort of Bible.

The theory of nature's significance in the development and education of children is exemplified in the *Père Castor* album series 'Le Roman des Bêtes' which illustrates parallels between the behaviour of children and that of various animals.[5] For instance, in *Bourru l'ours brun* children may – and should – see a lesson in the art of listening, smelling, climbing, eating properly, digging, striving, swimming and running.

A great many books about animals have been published since Kipling, but the scope of the genre is limited. Although some outstanding works have been written, there is not much variety. There are books based entirely on scientific observation which claim a certain authority such as *Les Souvenirs d'un entomologiste* (1879–1907) by Jean-Henri

4. *The Jungle Books.*
5. Flammarion. The first of this series is *Panache l'Ecureuil* (1934).

Fabre, Maeterlinck's *Le trésor des humbles*, *La vie des abeilles*, *La vie des fourmis* etc., which have inspired many writers. In *Magasin d'éducation et de récréation*, parodies of Fabre have appeared, like *La Gileppe*, *les infortunes d'une population d'insectes* by Dr Candize, but the only good contemporary writer in this vein is the German Waldemar Bonsels with *Die Biene Maja* and *Mario, ein Leben im Walde*.

Then there are essays in animal psychology such as those by the American writers Jack London, Oliver Curwood and Ernest Seton, the Russian Vitali Bianki, or Alberto Manzi, whose *Castor Grogh et sa tribu* is the most successful in a difficult genre. Finally there are stories about the relationship between men and animals which are as varied as they are numerous: *Tarzan of the Apes* by Edgar Rice Burroughs, the novels of Fred Gipson, Mary O'Hara and Marjorie Rawlings in the U.S.A.; Anna Sewell and Eric Knight in Great Britain; in France, stories by René Guillot, and Joseph Kessel's beautiful book *Le Lion*. This list cannot hope to be exhaustive because so many are published each year relating the passionate attachment of a child to a horse, a lion-cub, a bear-cub, a guinea-pig etc. Such books tend to be over-literary and to indulge in obsessive verbosity and lyricism – especially as there is little dramatic scope apart from the well-worn tear-jerker of the child refusing to part from his beloved companion. René Guillot, in his bush and jungle tales, seldom succeeds in equalling Kipling's restraint and vigour.

Animal books for children are a good example of trading on popular subject-matter and literary gimmickry. Starting from the proposition that children are fond of animals, writers lost no time in exploiting the vein. All children pass through an animal phase: animals are ideal partners and accomplices, their presence at the side of the little hero enhances his reality in the reader's eyes and all the author has to do is make the companion life-like. To do this he must find out what the child really expects from the animal and what sort of satisfaction he derives from its adventures. There is the partnership with a being who, like himself, is an outsider, yet in front of whom he can show off, like Mowgli. He is not a man, but he can exert his will on the animal and discover himself as a 'man-cub', and feel physical pleasure in the animal's vitality, but these are not the most important elements. The animal story is a pretext for the invention of a free society based on different relationships from those which are familiar to children; they are submitted to constraints and prohibitions from an early age and learn only too quickly that treats usually end in tears and regrets, but there is always the possibility that the same rules do not apply in the world of animals. As an intruder in the animal societies of his books, the child has the unique experience of perfect psychological balance. When instinct overruled desire and constrained Mowgli to go back to the society of his fellow men, he was stricken with such grief that he thought he was about to die. Very much the same thing happened to Nils Holgersson when he was finally released from the spell and became a little boy once again but, in consequence, lost the faculty he had possessed as a troll to understand animal language, and had to abandon his friends:

When he had reached the top of the hill he turned round and gazed at the flocks of birds starting off on their journey across the seas. They were all emitting their distinctive cries; only a flock of wild duck flew in silence for as long as his eyes could follow them.

But their triangular formation was in perfect order – distances properly maintained, speed adequate and wing-beats powerful and regular. Nils felt such a violent rush of regret that he almost wished he could be a midget again and travel over land and sea with a flock of wild duck.

Nils is left with his regrets while the ducks pursue their

regular lives, as rhythmic and orderly as their migration and the formation of their flight. For both Nils and Mowgli, animal life symbolizes order – an order which is opposed to the absurdity of the adult world ruled by illogical, groundless, incomprehensible laws:

... [Mowgli] was so busy learning the ways and customs of men. First he had to wear a cloth round him, which annoyed him horribly; and then he had to learn about money, which he did not in the least understand, and about ploughing, of which he did not see the use ... [6]

The perfect balance of animal societies rests on inexorable natural law: the necessity of every action is its perfect justification. Children try to evade the uncongenial adult world by adopting a disguise which makes them feel they are different, or by taking refuge in the animal world – like Delphine and Marinette with the farm animals – where they are safe from the perpetual interference of adults in their games, and insured against the absurd moral and social conventions which always disturb the harmony of their emotional relationships.

This is, in fact, their ideal of happiness and some of the best animal stories offer precisely this image of a possible earthly paradise. The early *Babar* books fall short of this ideal only because they lack a certain boldness and are slightly too dependent on moral and social norms, too close to reality, in fact. Among the books which do succeed in conveying this passionate relish in all things good and beautiful are *The Wind in the Willows* by Kenneth Grahame – which has coloured the dreams of every English child for the past sixty years or so – and a recent work by the American poet and critic Randall Jarrell, *Animal Family*. An atmosphere of total security and unadulterated bliss dominates the world of Kenneth Grahame's innocent little

6. *The Jungle Book*, London, 1894, p. 71.

beasts: Mole, Water-Rat, Toad, Badger etc., as well as that of the strange family imagined by Randall Jarrell which includes an old trapper, a lynx, a bear, a mermaid and a little boy. This is what life might have been like, were it not what it is. There are few pages of children's literature which give so total an impression of physical satisfaction and mental tranquillity as the first chapter of *The Wind in the Willows* with Toad and Water-Rat rowing on the river. Yet these two happy books are strangely sad. For the reader – even the child reader – knows that the blissful existence on the river-bank or in the trapper's hut with brother lynx and mother mermaid is an impossible Utopia. The child disguises itself – but the disguise is an illusion which must be discarded – he must give up the animal world and the baby world as well and see himself for what he is: a child, naked and exposed in a universe of real men and children, not of dream figures, toys, puppets and animals.

7. *The Home*

Now that the subject of disguise has been explored we may well ask who are the real heroes of children's books? The child-heroes of didactic literature in the eighteenth and early nineteenth centuries were neither convincing nor distinctive; they were vague figures without any specific characteristics. Rousseau discovered and explored the world of childhood, insisted that adequate attention be given to children's abilities and needs, but for nearly a century real human children continued to be virtually excluded from both adult and children's literatures. Was it because, while demanding that the child's physical, intellectual and emotional requirements be taken into consideration, Rousseau failed to evoke a convincing picture of children as beings capable of individual experience. Many of the child-heroes in eighteenth- and nineteenth-century children's literature refused to come to life; they were beings who never grew any older, never developed, never underwent real experience. They had no freedom of action or sensitivity and appeared to respond only to exterior motivations. They were mere pretexts, especially in didactic books, and, to a certain extent, even in folk tales, only used as catalysts introduced into the narrative to ensure the success of the story. They reacted either to a transcendental moral code or were the prey of impulses or the author's whim.

There are, of course, exceptions to this generalization; the

lively families in the books of Charlotte Yonge, each individual distinct from the others, the four heroines of Louisa
Alcott's *Little Women*; and on a lower level the two naughty
children of Catherine Sinclair's *Holiday House*, are all
recognizable characters with their own personalities, habits
and possibilities of change and development. But in the
general run of children's books the characters were sub-
ordinate to the unfolding of a plot, its vicissitudes and
adventures, its moral and poetic implications; they totally
lacked the one essential condition for existence, an individuality. Even late nineteenth- and early twentieth-century
characters such as Alice and Peter Pan had only their names
to distinguish them: they possessed no other identity, and
absolutely nothing was said about who they were or where
they came from. More often than not they would be a group
of children such as Nesbit's Five Children, but no one
individual emerged with idiosyncrasies which precluded his
being taken for anybody else.

Oliver Twist is probably the first real child-hero of
children's literature and he bursts into the novel as suddenly
as life itself:

For a long time after it was ushered into this world of sorrow
and trouble by the parish surgeon, it remained a matter of con-
siderable doubt whether the child would survive to bear any
name at all; in which case it is somewhat more than probable
that these memoirs would never have appeared; or if they had,
that being comprised within a couple of pages, they would have
possessed the inestimable merit of being the most concise and
faithful specimen of biography in the literature of any age or
country. Although I am not disposed to maintain that the being
born in a workhouse is in itself the most fortunate and enviable
circumstance that can possibly befall a human being, I do mean
to say that in this particular instance it was the best thing for
Oliver Twist that could by possibility have occurred ... Now,
if, during this brief period Oliver had been surrounded by careful grandmothers, anxious aunts, experienced nurses, and

doctors of profound wisdom he would most inevitably and indubitably have been killed in no time. There being nobody by, however, but a pauper old woman, who was rendered rather misty by an unwonted allowance of beer; and a parish surgeon who did such matters by contract; Oliver and Nature fought out the point between them.

While this opening expresses the irrepressible absurdity of existence, it also illustrates the difficulty of bringing an unusual hero to life. Indeed readers who were used to the conventional characters of picaresque or drawing-room novels would take some persuading before they became involved in the fate of a workhouse orphan. In their view a child had, at best, not much to recommend it as a hero, and here, into the bargain, was a proletarian child – a completely unromantic species . . .

The reader's interest and involvement in a fictional hero's existence depends on the character's emotional potential – that is to say, his tribulations. As long as errors and deficiencies of education were the child's only claim to social reorganization and to public attention, there could be no child-heroes in literature. Rousseau himself admitted that eighteenth-century children were not unhappy; the trouble was that they were brought up according to irrational principles, which is a very different matter – and this was only true of upper-class children anyhow; the others, the little peasants who roamed the mountains and the country-side had all the contact with nature anyone could wish them; their lungs were filled with fresh air, their muscles were exercised and they enjoyed the rough and ready, if rather primitive affection of their parents – which had the advantage of being lively and spontaneous. It was not until children were seen to be victims at the hands of their seniors that the fictional child-hero stood a chance of coming alive.

In France in 1840 Villermé published the *Tableau de l'état physique et moral des ouvriers employés dans les manufactures de coton, de laine et de soie* which revealed the extent of childhood's victimization.

In both these industries, that of wool and that of cotton, children are, in fact, required only as machine-minders. However, in all cases, their protracted working hours are exhausting. They are made to stand for sixteen to seventeen hours each day, of which thirteen are spent shut up in a room where they barely have space enough to move or stretch their limbs. This is not a task or an employment, it is sheer torture; and it is inflicted upon under-fed, inadequately clothed six-to-eight-year-olds who must set out at five o'clock in the morning to reach the factory in time . . .

and ill-treatment is added to torture:

. . . when the poor little mites are overcome with fatigue and drop off to sleep they are woken up by any available means – which does not exclude the strap.

Forced labour, the crime committed against childhood in all nineteenth-century industrialized countries, turned the child into a object of pity. What Dickens experienced as a child briefly in the flesh became romanticized and was translated into the literary world in the persons of Oliver Twist and David Copperfield. Victor Hugo created Cosette and Gavroche. Dickens's and Hugo's reaction of generous indignation gave rise to the image of a 'tender being still warm from its mother's body and hardly yet weaned from her breast, asking nothing more than to be allowed to blossom forth into flower'.[1] The lyricism of the expression indicates a new attitude which, although inspired by Rousseau's 'Let childhood ripen in children', is less detached and more emotional, nay sentimental: nineteenth-century artists were bent at all costs on recovering a true image of childhood; they could not bear to think of children suffering and martyred and they took society to task for oppressing

1. Michelet, op. cit., Part II, chapter 4.

this most fragile and vulnerable portion of humanity. Thus, life-like, strongly individualized fictional characters emerged and to those already named we may add such heroes as Jacques Vingtras, Huckleberry Finn and all the other children and adolescents of literature who knew what lay in store for them and were prepared to fight for their rights.

Between *Oliver Twist* in 1838 and *Huckleberry Finn* in 1884 a number of writers – among them Victor Hugo, George Sand, Michelet, Erckmann, Chatrian and Vallès – raised a united voice in defence of children and in protest against the shameful conditions of their existence. They all had one thing in common and this was an emotional fixation on the phenomenon of childhood: 'I have made it a rule in my life never to trust anyone who tells me he is not interested in children', Dickens declared in a speech he made in 1858 for the endowment of a children's hospital. Steeped in Rousseau's theories, they were particularly susceptible to the pitiful injustice of children's lives and tended to think in symbols, accommodating their own personal mystique to the lofty, generous ideals of the century of progress, distinguished by its faith in the future of mankind; they believed that, guided by the 'Angel of Liberty' and the 'Great Enlightenment', 'the People' would finally emerge from social squalor and the shadows of obscurantism. They unconsciously identified children and the people: ' . . . No, childhood is not merely an age, a stage of existence, it is a people, an innocent people . . . '[2]

Children had their rights as the people had theirs and it was the duty of writers and philosophers to defend them and to prevent 'the child from becoming atrophied by darkness' as Victor Hugo says in his preface to *Les Misérables*. Children had first to be saved from the calamities of poverty, then enlightened by education. However, certain anxieties began to be felt and when a member of the Com-

2. Michelet, op. cit., Part V, chapter 4.

mune, Vallès, followed up his declaration: 'I shall defend the *rights of children* as others defend the *rights of man*', with the significant words: 'I shall question the father's right of life and death over his child's body and soul',[3] he showed that he had considered the conditions in which children lived with more realism and less optimism than his well-intentioned, liberal, middle-class contemporaries. For romantics were unanimous in their conviction that children could not blossom out and develop normally if they were deprived of emotional stability; that is to say, that children should be allowed to grow up in the midst of the family and one of their main grievances against industrial societies was that they deprived children of this advantage. Dickens and Victor Hugo – and to a lesser degree George Sand and Erckmann and Chatrian – idealized family life and the home, which Dickens represented as the 'Christmas Spirit'. Parallel themes were those of motherhood and adoption, the corner-stone of *Les Misérables*.

Some of these idealists did concede that children might be permitted to venture from the warmth and intimacy of their homes, as long as it was for the no less secure and sheltered sanctuary of the school, where they would attend to the inspiring words, falling from the lips of 'the Master'. But here too there was room for dissension. Thus Vallès dedicates L'Enfant:

To all those who were bored to death in class and made to cry at home, who, during their childhood were bullied by their teachers and beaten by their parents ...

and Dickens' portraits of school life in *Nicholas Nickleby* and *David Copperfield* are quite horrific.

If the end to be achieved is the free development of children, one must consider the constraints imposed by the home and the school. Though these threats to the blossoming

3. Jules Vallès, *L'Enfant*, 1878.

forth of the child did not receive much attention in Latin countries, they inspired a number of English and American writers. For instance Mark Twain, in his two novels for and about adolescents – *Tom Sawyer* and *Huckleberry Finn* – denounced Puritan hypocrisy and advocated a freedom of action and thought which could only be realized outside the influence of home and school. Indeed, apart from his right to health, care and education, a child is also entitled to freedom.

All these theories, however, which we can mention only briefly here, were expressed by writers who did not specialize in children's books. They wrote for a wide public and primarily for the people; but since, in the nineteenth century, a great flood of popular and children's literature burst forth, consisting of an indiscriminate medley of serial stories, pamphlets, reminiscences, manifestoes etc., these very widely circulated works easily became children's favourites, and have, in fact, acquired a place for themselves among children's classics.*

How did the authors who wrote exclusively for children use contemporary themes? How did the increasing number of books about children evolve and develop? The first great realistic novels for children were not published till some twenty years after *Oliver Twist*. Madame de Ségur began to write in 1857; Louisa Alcott's *Little Women* appeared in 1867; Mark Twain's *The Adventures of Tom Sawyer* in 1876 and *Sans Famille* by Hector Malot in 1878. As a matter of fact, the publication of realistic children's books appears to have been restricted to three distinct periods dating roughly from 1860 to 1900; from 1930 to 1940; and from about ten years ago till the present date.

* Editor's note: An example of books not primarily written for children but which have become children's classics through their appeal to the young of most ages, are *The Christmas Carol*, parts of *Oliver Twist*, parts of *David Copperfield* and, of course, the outstanding cases of *Robinson Crusoe* and *Gulliver's Travels*.

Unlike Hugo's Gavroche or the characters in the novels written by Erckmann and Chatrian, who were all working-class children, the heroes of these later stories usually came from well-to-do families unexpectedly reduced to poverty by some reverse of fortune; indeed, the working-class child seems to have become remarkably unpopular as a hero and it must be admitted that the theme of poverty is pleasanter – or at least more easily acceptable – when approached indirectly. That is why such reassuring stories as *The Little Princess* by Frances Hodgson Burnett, for instance, were so popular. Here, owing to unforeseen circumstances – the father's death, an unfortunate business enterprise and bankruptcy – the rich, pampered little girl becomes a beggar and experiences real poverty until the miracle occurs in the form of her guardian, an elderly invalid gentleman, who finally discovers her whereabouts and restores her to her former happy existence. In this way little peasants or labourers and later working-class children, isolated from any distinct environment, are represented by the symbolic figure of the 'poor child' standing for misfortune in general.

Some books do, however, portray more or less faithfully the little proletarian child's circumstances. Among these is *Froggy's Little Brother* by 'Brenda' where uncompromising realism mingles with sentimentality very much in the manner of Dickens. It is the most characteristic of the 'street arab' stories, and only in this sort of fiction was any attempt made to portray the lives of the urban poor and the wretchedness of children lost in the slums, living in fear of the ultimate horror of the workhouse. The most convincing working-class child-heroes are possibly those of Hector Malot[4] and especially those imagined by the very reactionary Comtesse de Ségur, some of whose novels are, in fact so well documented and the characters so realistically portrayed

4. *Sans Famille*, the mining episode; *En Famille*, the young factory-girls in the northern spinning mills.

4

in their true social circumstances that they might be classed among sociological works. Madame de Ségur's keen sense of observation, her thoroughness and her argumentativeness inclined her to inquire into problems of economic inequality. Her manner of handling a character to bring him to life expresses her partiality for material detail and her remarkable statistical sense, two qualities which made her into a sociologist before sociology was invented.5 It is thanks to the novels of the *Bibliòtheque rose* that we can tell what a nurse-maid received as wages, how much she could make on the side in gifts and tips, what she was given in kind, how many dresses she possessed and what she spent on foot-wear. And from *Diloy le chemineau* on – in such books as *Jean qui grogne et Jean qui rit*, *La Soeur de Gribouille*, *La fortune de Gaspard* and *Le bon génie* – we find a complete inventory of working-children's conditions and wages. Here, for example, are some children in a workshop:

Diloy: It's a job in a slipper-workshop, sir; I get bed and board and two francs fifty a day.

The General: And how many hours is the working day?

Diloy: Twelve, sir.

The General: That's two too many. Do you have Sundays and holidays off?

Diloy: Depends. I could be told to stay and work when orders are behind.

The General: And orders will always be behind for these manufacturing gentlemen. And what about children? Are there any employed there?

Diloy: Ten-year-olds work for fifty centimes a day sir.

The General: And is it tiring, difficult work?

Diloy: 'Tisn't too bad but they have to sit still all the time.

The General: And do these children work out in the open?

Diloy: No, sir, in the workshop; they never go out.

5. Cf. Pierre Bleton, *La Vie sociale dans le second Empire, un étonnant témoignage de la Comtesse de Ségur*, Éditions ouvrières, Paris, 1963.

The General: And do they have Sundays off? Are they able to go to Sunday School and to attend school during the week?
Diloy: Not when they are needed.
The General: And of course they are always needed.

In *Jean qui grogne et Jean qui rit* we are told about the working conditions of a grocer's boy and a thirteen-year-old café waiter:

I promised Simon you'd have ten francs, uniform, board, lodging and washing. Watch out the ten francs don't all go for breakages.

Madame de Ségur describes all the practical and moral differences between a young factory foreman,[6] a little seamstress[7] and a page-boy in an upper-class establishment[8] as well as the countless peasant children she describes at their work in the fields or at school, stuffing at the village fête or subsisting on an unvarying diet which varies from being frugal in the rich Norman countryside to being miserably inadequate in impoverished Brittany.

Madame de Ségur does not only state facts; she relates them to their psychological consequences; if the proletarian child is not like the upper- or middle-class child it is because he has to work for his living on a scanty, unhealthy diet. But he is also completely different in his psychological make-up. This fact is illustrated in the following dialogue between the hall-porter's son and the little master:

'That elephant must cost a tidy sum to feed,' said Blaise. 'He eats at one meal as much as Mum, Dad and me eat in a week.'
Jules: 'But can't you see that he doesn't eat any meat? You have to eat meat to keep alive, haven't you?'

6. *La Fortune de Gaspard.*
7. *La Soeur de Gribouille.*
8. *Jean qui grogne et Jean qui rit.*

Blaise: 'Meat, Master Jules! We never eat meat except on Sundays, and not much even then; why, a joint no bigger than my fist lasts us for Monday dinner as well!'

'Well, I never!' exclaimed Jules. 'I don't eat anything but meat. But what do you eat on weekdays then?'

Blaise: 'Cheese, a hard-boiled egg, some vegetables ... and bread, of course, I can have as much bread as I like.'

Jules: 'Oh well, I can tell you that if they didn't give me any meat I just wouldn't eat.'

Blaise: 'It would be the worse for you, Master Jules, because you'd go hungry; and when you're hungry everything tastes good ... '[9]

The theme of mortification runs through Madame de Ségur's work like a *leit-motif* and serves as an outlet for her sadistic instincts – the wicked, the vain and the 'sinful rich' are all humbled in the end – but it is mainly expressed in her descriptions of social relations for, if, in her stories, the clash of personalities appears to be based on moral principles and to illustrate differences of temperament, it is in reality the result of social distinctions. Though her early works – especially the Sophie collection[10] – are moral tales for good children in the manner of Berquin, and all the characters have the same social background – sensible Camille at loggerheads with unruly Sophie and cowardly Léon overcome by brave Paul – further contrasts soon intervene: clumsy, ostentatious Simplicie is handicapped by her ill-breeding in the drawing-room of her Parisian friends, well-behaved 'exemplary' little girls who do everything with aristocratic ease and elegance.[11] Félicie's behaviour is entirely conditioned by class-consciousness; in her conversations with her friends, the de Castelsots, and in her letters to them she is mainly pre-occupied with how she should address the servants or the peasants; another of these

9. *Pauvre Blaise.*
10. *Les malheurs de Sophie, Les petites Filles modèles, Les Vacances.*
11. *Les deux nigauds.*

young ladies' obsessions is with wearing the right frock for the right occasion: 'My dear Félicie, let me know if you are going to wear a silk frock or a simple white one at the Robillard wedding'.[12] Madame de Ségur is naturally critical of such frivolity; but she lays great store by the subtle emotional gradations which correspond to differences of social background. Feelings are classed according to a basic scale of material benefits; the wealthy are generous and are moved and overjoyed when their generosity is suitably acknowledged, whereas the lot of the needy is humility, fear and gratitude ... The highly moral characters who represent the author's own attitude are extremely punctilious where such gradations are concerned; they know, for instance, that a person from the higher spheres of society may take part in popular rejoicings and even find them pleasurable – the lords of the Manor do not shun the village fête[13] and even condescend most becomingly to eat for once off rough tableware[14] but the lower classes, on the other hand, must never join the parties given by their superiors; on such occasions they should always know their place – which is that of a servant, though it can, if need be, become that of saviour. When Diloy or some other attendant goes fishing with the children it is not to take part in their sport, but only to bait their lines for them ... and save them from drowning. Such differentiation expresses a very pertinent view of complex bourgeois society which is rare in nineteenth- and even twentieth-century books for children. It is paradoxical that the effects of class conflict should be best illustrated by the Comtesse de Ségur, though she herself – loyal friend of Veuillot and mother of the Monsignor de Ségur later vilified by Victor Hugo – doubtless did not realize it.

12. *Diloy le chemineau.*
13. ibid.
14. *Pauvre Blaise.*

Faithful representations of society cannot be found in subsequent psychological and so-called realistic children's novels until the 1930s and this applies to all countries but specially to France. There seems to have been a halt, if not indeed a regression, in this particular field during the fifty years which separate Hector Malot from Charles Vildrac.

While Vallès was writing his trilogy there were no claims or protests in children's literature. The spirit of revolt had died out, but so had objective description. At best there was an attempt to awaken in children from bourgeois families an awareness of the conditions in which other classes of the population lived. It was not the proletarian condition itself that was stressed with its attendant alienation and neglect, but the most spectacular attributes, wretchedness and poverty which became a favourite literary theme; thus, as in the story of *The Little Princess*, heroes and heroines experienced poverty isolated from its social context. Once the working classes had ceased to starve, and class distinctions were not so much a matter of economics as a social, moral and intellectual problem, the popular figure of the 'beggar-child' lost the little reality it had and became nothing but a dramatic gimmick. As a result these would-be realistic novels made very little impression on public conscience and did nothing to alter social institutions. Far from being instruments of rebellion they remained well within the limits of a vague humanitarianism, something that might be described as watered-down Dickens, and he himself was not essentially a rebel.

In France this attitude can be attributed to Hetzel and Jean Macé's *Magasin d'education et de récréation* – or to the fact that the intellectual classes were for the most part schoolmasters who came to power under the Third Republic and adopted and interpreted to their own advantage the generous ideals of the 1848 revolutionaries. Naturally enough these men tried to impose their values on children. But apart from a Republican ideal and the united efforts of a parliamentary democracy against Napoleon III's despotism, these values were still those of the Second Empire bourgeois society whose staunchest upholders these new men turned out to be. *Magasin d'éducation et de récréation* was founded in 1864 by schoolteachers, liberals and the opponents of Napoleon III; but it was really the organ of all the old bourgeois principles. Literacy was seen as the magic cure-all, the cult of culture replacing that of noble birth, and the type of citizen it hoped to fashion was far from original but bore the indelible mark of class distinctions. Children were told about scholars, soldiers and labourers – though these were now promoted to the rank of farmers and craftsmen, while real workmen were ignored; they were urged to train for such careers as engineering, teaching, civil service or the army.

In 1871 Hetzel published *Les Grandes Écoles de France* by Mortimer d'Ocagne, in two volumes, one for military schools and one for lay schools, to help the young readers of *Magasin d'éducation et de récréation* to choose an appropriate vocation. If there had been any doubt as to the class of public to whom such literature was addressed, this was now definitely dispelled, for the cost of keeping a boy in one of these 'institutions of specialized education' was enormous. Furthermore the patriotism expressed by all its contributors reflected a self-satisfied, self-assured society. Authentic problems were never discussed, but tactfully ignored, while education was the one great hope that would set everything right in the future. Poverty became picturesque in the work of such writers as Hector Malot whose beggars were disguised as gypsies, and workmen just did not exist. To be conscious of the dignity of his task, a manual worker must be directly involved with his material, a peasant following the rhythm of the seasons and closely associated with nature. Craftsmen producing an object from start to finish, can reach self-fulfilment in their work, but the factory worker or the miner, slaving away at some obscure, fragmentary task cannot possibly symbolize the dignity of labour or be taken to express the satisfaction derived from a job well done. Not that work was not idealized on every page of *Magasin d'éducation et de récréation* and to emphasize its respectability any connection between work and profit was avoided. The result was a highly moral attitude to work and a professional hierarchy which was stressed in almost every article or story. A typical example is the following passage from *Marchand d'allumettes* by Gennevraye:

'So the trade you liked best, Sergeant, was that of soldier?'
'To begin with, lad, it isn't a trade, it's a profession.'
'What's the difference between a trade and a profession?'
'Well, you see . . . you see . . . ' and the Sergeant tried in vain to find the right words. At last his face lit up: 'A trade, Zidore, is what helps you to earn money; a profession is what helps you to achieve honour; that's the military profession!'[15]

In a lower key and a more vulgar tonality this passage echoes Péguy's imprecations against socialism for debasing the idea of work.

While a certain paternalism is an accepted part of Madame de Ségur's work, it seems quite out of place in the writers who contributed to *Magasin d'éducation et de récréation*. For instance, the wife of Fouillé, the philosopher, wrote two books which appeared in this collection under the penname of Bruno: *Le Tour de France de deux enfants* and *Francinet*; the latter depicts a situation which might well have arisen in one of the Countess's stories, though the style is unquestionably inferior. This is the relationship between a child factory-worker and the factory owner's

15. *Marchand d'allumettes* by A. Gennevraye in *Magasin d'éducation et de récréation*, 1 September, 1889, p. 108.

little daughter. Francinet envies the rich little girl who can play while he has to work – for which unnatural feelings he is severely censured by the author. However, the wealthy child assists the poor one in bettering his soul by teaching him the significance of renunciation; he finally understands that 'work is a form of prayer' and happily intones the 'song of the poor'.

> From the cot to the shroud
> My chain of toil is grievous!
> But labour makes a heart proud –
> With idleness it grows timorous

Moreover, he realizes that a wealthy manufacturer owes his position to a life of toil and hardship and that the little girl's father has thus earned, for himself and his family, the right to enjoy the fruits of his labours in ease and leisure . . .

Such, then, was the attitude expressed in one of the most popular primary school readers of the time and a great favourite among schoolteachers; an attitude which could not be more different from that of Vallès, Victor Hugo or George Sand, and which was totally unrealistic into the bargain, especially in its paternalism. These books, however, did not depict poor children's lives as easy; the poor, it had to be admitted, did suffer. But the basic problems of social constraint and inequality were never dealt with openly; the proletarian child was never set apart as a result of his social condition, it was always for some other equally dramatic and equally alienating reason. Hence all the little invalids and cripples whose condition was pathetic without being disturbing. Perhaps the only writer to infuse any life into this theme was Frances Hodgson Burnett in *The Secret Garden*, a novel that still seems advanced, at least in its treatment of children's illness. The heroes' maladies are not seen as being simply physical in cause: both children have been indulged without being loved; one reacts by

4*

hating everyone (including herself) and the other with fear and an abnormal shrinking from society.[16]

Social reality was not revived in children's literature until 1935; a fact which, in itself, is not surprising but the revival was half-hearted, never giving rise in this period to feelings of overt social rebellion against the *status quo*. However, it is possible to find faithful representations of working-class neighbourhoods in the novels of Charles Vildrac, Colette Vivier, Georges Nigremont, Marianne Monestier and Paul Berna in France; Eve Garnett, J. R. Townsend and William Mayne (mainly rural working-class life) in Britain, and in Germany in those of Herta von Ghebardt. Also worth mentioning are the American writer Lois Lenski, the Swede Harry Kullmann, the Italian, Mario Comassi, the Dutch writer Annie Winkler-Vonk and the Spaniard, Ana-Maria Matute.

Only two children's books come to mind where society is observed from an active political standpoint rather than from a purely ethical one. These are *A Pál Utcai Fiùk* ('The Paul Street boys) by Ferenc Molnar (1906) and *King Mathias I* by Janusz Korczak (1928) which both illustrate the basic contradictions between the adult world and the conception children have of it. The boys of Paul Street play at war and in the process they become so completely militarized that their whole attitude is changed; they break off their former confidential friendly relationships and finally bring about an actual state of conflict. However, this is only a make-believe war without any serious consequences and it ends abruptly as soon as the adults intervene. The

16. The theme has recently made a reappearance in American children's literature. Writers are concentrating on children who are 'not like the others' (invalids, handicapped children of all types, 'exceptional children' and immigrants and racial minorities) and this points once again to feelings of malaise among the American intelligentsia. The movement seems not so much an attempt to salve an uneasy conscience, however, as a genuine breaking down of a longstanding taboo.

adults are, in fact, responsible for the disappearance of the bone of contention – a stretch of waste-land claimed by two rival gangs, both unaware that it has already been selected as a building-site by speculators. Since the territory for which the two bands of boys were contending already belonged to a third party there was no more cause for conflict and the mustering of all these youthful energies had really been pointless from the start; nonetheless, something did in fact happen which momentarily transformed a group of harmless children into a threatening, insensitive mob.

King Mathias I describes a child-community and children living independently. It raises the problem of the feasibility and the consequences of such a community. *The Paul Street Boys* is essentially a novel, *King Mathias I* is more of a parable. These two authoritative, deeply original works and also, perhaps, Mark Twain's *The Prince and the Pauper* are the only books to set before young readers authentic political problems, but there are other books in which child communities play a prominent part. These are, of course, the books about school life which were so popular in the nineteenth century.

Nowadays, however, there are relatively few school stories compared to the vast output of fairy tales, stories about family life and adventure stories.* In the nineteenth century there was a tendency to idealize school life; *Magasin d'éducation et de récréation* published a much-read series by André Laurie which described the activities of schoolchildren in schools all the world over. The most striking example of such an attitude is *Cuore* by Edmondo de Amicis. It should be remembered, by the way, that most of these

* Editor's note: There has certainly been in this country a new style of school story, notably those written by William Mayne and Mary Harris. The Jennings stories by Anthony Buckeridge conform more to the older style which Mlle Jan dismisses from the contemporary scene.

books were written by schoolmasters who – in France, perhaps more than elsewhere – had only just won a hard battle in the field of education; they were sincerely convinced that democracy was based on the secular schools available to all which they themselves were founding, that those schools were the very symbol of democracy, its alpha and omega. They could not really be expected to perceive their own shortcomings or to make fun of a project upon which they were still lavishing so much enthusiasm and energy. Once the system had been solidly established the tone changed; jokes were permitted, the masters' quirks might be affectionately ridiculed and the young hero could play tricks on the school authorities – who were never authoritarian, but neither were the pupils ever really reprehensible. In France the series *Le Petit Nicolas* by Sempé and Goscinny, and in England the stories of the schoolboy *Jennings* by Anthony Buckeridge today enjoy a well-deserved popularity if only because they have revived the old tradition of ragging – a ritualistic, and therefore harmless, method of challenging authority. In fact, what these stories illustrate is really no more than youthful high spirits and the art of letting off steam without any serious consequences, but school as such is never criticized: the teaching function or the content of lessons are never mocked.

The voice of Vallès contrasting the deadening effects of education with life itself and deploring the sad fate of all 'those who were fed on Greek and Latin but died of starvation'[17] continues to fall on deaf ears. Primary and secondary schools are still generally represented in a very idealized form and even the most realistic authors somehow fail to be realistic when describing these institutions. One wonders what school memories live on in adult minds! There are nonetheless a few exceptions; Léonce Bourliaguet's early novel *Quatre au cours moyen*, Pierre Gamarra's *Le Mystère de la*

17. Cf. the dedication of *Bachelier*.

Berlurette, Paul Berna's novels and especially those by Colette Vivier are more or less faithful portrayals of school life; however, these books tend to describe village schools, thoroughly integrated into community life and surrounded by fields and woods, which lends them an aura of poetry so that they constitute, in fact, a very literary and nostalgic genre, half-way between *Le Grand Meaulnes* and *La Guerre des boutons*.

But if school stories lack authenticity, writers have always tried to give a feeling of reality to their descriptions of home. Home is a child's life, the bright centre to which he is instinctively drawn and which haunts his dreams when it is out of reach. Thus it is probably not an accident that in *Sans Famille*'s opening chapter we see Rémi tossing pancakes by the fireside with kindly Mother Barberin, and that *Little Women* by Louisa Alcott opens with the four sisters chatting by the fireside. Charlotte M. Yonge was one of the first and most prolific writers of family stories and her interminable sagas were eagerly awaited by readers of all ages. Her reputation, however, has not lasted and *Little Women* remains as the archetype of the family story – a genre which evokes all the warm, comforting permanence of family ties and of shared domestic tasks. The 'family story' imbues everyday life with an aura of poetry.

In such stories parents are models whose broadminded, understanding attitude can sometimes be strict. There is always an old, devoted but cantankerous retainer who willingly foregoes her wages when the family find themselves temporarily in straitened circumstances. Brothers and sisters live together in perfect harmony, the odd quarrel only serving to enhance their basic solidarity. All of this is in striking opposition to the tradition of folk tales where family misunderstandings always play a prominent part; where parents favour one particular child, brothers and sisters envy one another and children are ejected from their homes or ill-treated. In fact the only feature of this tradition to have been retained by the family story is that of the step-mother and even this is turned upside-down. For where in popular tales the cruel step-mother rejects the child and is duly punished for her wickedness in the end, in the realistic novel the child – influenced, perhaps, by too many fairy tales – rejects the step-mother. However, all ends well here and the step-mother wins over the child's affections by sheer devotion and patience, which goes to prove that life is not a fairy tale; it is better than all the fairy tales put together . . . The one exception to this rule is Madame Fichini in *Les petites Filles modèles* whose only departure from the traditional fairy-story, step-mother role is her final repentance before the inevitable punishment – but then concessions had to be made to strict Roman Catholic principles . . .

Alongside the 'family story', however, we find some books by English or American authors about unhappy homes which are mostly a form of protest against Protestant puritanism. Since Mark Twain, a number of writers have denounced the stifling effects of such principles on the normal development of children, and particularly the notion of original sin from which these innocent beings are supposed to suffer. Indeed, this essentially American theme which Melville and Hawthorne interpreted with supreme mastery, runs – albeit in a minor key – through children's literature as well. It forms the backbone of Kate Wiggin's beautiful novel *Rebecca of Sunnybrook Farm* (1902) where Rebecca is brought up by her two narrow-minded, bigoted aunts who are disturbed by this youthful presence in their gloomy home and interpret all her qualities of sweetness, gaiety and beauty as manifestations of the evil and corruption inherent in human nature. But the tone is always light-hearted and witty and the author has sufficient consideration for young readers to make the old aunts finally relent. However the problem is adequately stated: though children may be impulsive and wayward they are fragile, inexperienced beings and they can suffer irreparable damage through the effects of harshness and the fanaticism of a moral code from which faith in mankind is excluded.

In this book adult incomprehension of children and its chilling effect on a child are made bearable by representing the conflict as between a niece and her aunts. And all the many books dealing with this subject display a similar tact in avoiding desecration of the parent-child relationship; thus the children are always committed to the care of grandparents, guardians, uncles, aunts or cousins. Few books analyse the parent-child relationship with any subtlety. Even in nineteenth-century novels parents were stereotypes devoid of personality; any liveliness there was derived from the servants or other adults while the presence of parents was purely utilitarian. Indeed, fathers were almost entirely absent from Madame de Ségur's novels, the mothers being widows or with husbands lost at sea – unless these gentlemen were simply 'taking the waters', while Louisa Alcott's Dr March was at the front with the army. Mothers were invariably beautiful, good and comforting though they were sometimes rather fragile, weak-willed creatures in the manner of Mrs Copperfield senior. Nowadays children are not so easily orphaned in fiction, but their parents still remain discreetly off-stage and are not permitted to intervene in any adventure and are definitely outside the story. Thus the exceptional tales in which these two essential characters play some part are worthy of note.

We find for instance in *Serioja* by Vera Panova a very delicate and interesting study of a little boy's relationship with his parents. Or a portrayal of pre-adolescent rebellion against a father in *It's like this, Cat* by Emily Neville – a novel which has affinities with Salinger's *Catcher in the Rye*, though it is much less forceful. Actually, the fallen-father figure is quite an obsession with American writers and the first of these sick, alcoholic, degraded progenitors is to be found, unexpectedly enough, in *Huckleberry Finn*, which is to all intents and purposes a book for children yet at the same time can be seen as the mainspring of the American novel. In no other book can we find anything to surpass the power and truth of certain passages on the relationship between father and son. We are shown, for instance, how the young Huckleberry is brought to the very brink of parricide by his disgust and rebellion:

> So he dozed off, pretty soon. By and by I got the old split-bottom chair and clumb up, as easy as I could, not to make any noise, and got down the gun. I slipped the ramrod down it to make sure it was loaded, and then I laid it across the turnip barrel, pointing towards Pop, and set down behind it to wait for him to stir. And how slow and still the time did drag along . . .

But the theme of the relationship between a son and his unworthy father was taken up only by adult writers; understandably enough it rarely figures in children's literature where accounts of such disturbing family circumstances are considered out of place. Until quite recently the broken home was taken as a subject in only one children's book, *Das doppelte Löttchen* (Lotte and Lisa)* by Eric Kästner. Here we are given a child's-eye view of the relationship between parents and the tragedy of their divorce, but Kästner resorts to fantasy and humour in order to make this subject acceptable. He gives his serious problem an improbable, whimsical tale, which he then organizes like a

* Editor's note: *Lotte and Lisa* by Erik Kästner has been succeeded in England and America by several books dealing sometimes specifically with broken homes, sometimes with a broken marriage as only one of a number of problems. It is interesting that in recent years very few of these books end with a reconciliation between the parents; it is much more usual now for the child to have to come to terms with the fact that the parents are going to stay apart and to recognize this as an increasingly common phenomenon in life. One recent example is *A Cat Called Camouflage* by Cordelia Jones published by Deutsch.

ballet, making use of doubles, substitute-children and all the devices of comedy; the parallel is further stressed by the fact that the story unfolds in the world of the theatre. This is perhaps the best novel by the author of *Emil and the Detectives*; it has the great merit of dealing with a serious subject and the further advantage of doing so without being ponderous; furthermore artists are depicted here in a realistic way – a rare achievement in children's literature where they usually appear as *deus ex machina* or a Father Christmas, crudely portrayed and with a total lack of conviction.

Eric Kästner probably chose the surest way of representing family conflicts objectively by adopting a humorous tone for his novel; his parents are repressive and stupidly authoritarian, their manners are often humiliating, their quarrels frequent and unpredictable, yet far from inciting to rebellion like Vallès or turning the situation into a tragedy like Jules Renard, he simply makes it funny. Children had already learnt to laugh at their parents and at themselves with Töpffer's *Monsieur Crépin* – whose absurd adventures with his eleven children have never been surpassed in anti-didactic literature – and with the comic strips: *Buster Brown*, *Bicot*, *Mac Magnus* etc. The most ridiculous family in literature is surely the family portrayed by Lucretia Hale in *Peterkin Papers* published in the American Magazine *Young Folks* in 1886, and a great favourite with American children for half a century. Here a family of puppets passes from one domestic crisis to another with a comic effect akin to that of silent film slapstick. However ridiculous they may be, Lucretia Hale's characters are never aggressive. In the widely read Italian classic, *Il giornalino di Gian Burrasca* by Vamba, which, alas, has never been translated, the child is possessed by a demon of destructiveness and spares neither individuals nor institutions. Parents, teachers and representatives of law and order also fall victim to his fury and diabolic ingenuity. Gian Burrasca is definitely a cousin of

Wilhelm Busch's two little wretches, Max and Moritz,[18] but the latter are cartoon characters who perpetrate mechanical farces whereas Vamba's jokes are closer to satire. Humour at the expense of family relationships is rarely very fierce, as a rule it is simply the necessary safety valve that maintains a happy balance in such relationships, so softening them and finally making them acceptable. Such is the conciliatory attitude adopted, for instance, by the excellent German writer Winterfeld in *Timpeltill*, an appealing story where parents react to their children's rebellion and cheek by a practical joke rather than in an authoritarian manner or by trying to appeal to their 'better natures'. They abdicate their rights and quietly depart, leaving the children to manage as best they can on their own in the little township of Timpeltill. Neither party wins in the end but each has had the opportunity to gauge its own potentialities, not in a melodramatic way but through an entertaining comedy.

Parent-child dialogue is represented with extreme delicacy in three works of unequal value but similar outlook which concentrate, on the relationship between a boy and his father or grandfather. These are: *Feuerschuh und Windsandal* by Ursula Wolfel, *Histoires du petit Père Renaud* by Leopold Chauveau and *Mein Urgrossvater und Ich* by James Krüss. The first is an unpretentious but effective work but the other two contribute something original to children's literature. All three tackle the subject from the same angle and with equal lack of constraint. The grown-up in these stories never behaves childishly or plays the fool, but gives free rein to the youthful impulses which survive in every adult – apart from a few rare specimens – and it is the adult who sweeps the child along with him from adventure to adventure, discovery to discovery and disaster to catastrophe; the child

18. In this context we must remember their famous predecessors, Struwwelpeter and all the characters created by Heinrich Hoffmann who were so cruelly punished for their misdeeds.

follows passively at first, but gradually participates in all these activities to the point where he rivals his parent's inventiveness, daring and uninhibited behaviour and thus a relationship of mutual confidence is firmly established. There are unfortunately too few children's books of this kind, perhaps because, in order to be plausible and avoid seeming contrived they require that rare combination of gifts possessed by Leopold Chauveau and James Krüss: an extreme delicacy of touch and a true perception of what children want.

There are many books which treat family problems seriously (and they do call for serious treatment). About three quarters of the novels written for boys and girls since 1850 tell the story of a lost, abandoned orphan child in search of a family; during one hundred and fifty pages or so he hunts for his mother and father and ends up having found them − or an adequate substitute. For a lonely, orphaned or neglected child is, indeed, lost in Tom Thumb's dark forest; he cannot believe that he will ever see daylight again; darkness will surround him for evermore like the child in Victor Hugo's *Les Misérables*:

'Your son is crying,' said Thenardier. 'Go and see what he wants.'

'Drat him!' answered the mother. 'I'm sick of him!'

And the neglected child continued to sob in the darkness.[19]

This most acute suffering gives rise to the most obstinate quest, and we should not smile at the contrived endings, the joyful reunions which inevitably await the orphan at the last page; they are not simply gimmicks to tie up the loose strands in children's literature but correspond to an essential need in the child-reader − and without detracting from the intensity of despair which precedes them. The story of the nestling fallen from its nest must, of necessity, end in the reassuring

19. Victor Hugo, *Les Misérables*, Part II, Book III, chapter 1.

comfort of reintegration. The hero has recovered a home and the reader has satisfied an unconscious desire to exchange his home.

Though the unconfessed dream of changing mothers and fathers is usually completely repressed, children often indulge the fantasy of having different sisters and brothers, cousins or godparents from those they really have; they adopt easily and let themselves be adopted. Moreover adoption, taken in its widest connotation, is probably the basic psychological theme in children's literature. It can be interpreted in many different ways and even grotesquely exaggerated as with Madame de Ségur's *General Dourakine*; a story where children acquire new brothers, cousins or guardians and where grown-ups are landed with children of another stock, allows for a great deal of emotional play. Because children's literature lacks the essential emotional outlet of erotic passion the feelings it describes are really more or less disguised and distorted substitutes for adult love; what we are given is a semblance, and a rather poor one at that. However, it would be unwise to elaborate *a priori* theories or form hasty opinions on this subject. If overt eroticism is naturally banished from children's books, passion is certainly not excluded and family relationships – once they have been extended to include the various possibilities that adoption has to offer – allow for the whole gamut of interchanges, emotional explorations and discoveries, rich in possibilities.*

In François le bossu, little Christine, who is at the centre of the story and upon whom all the thoughts, desires and

* Editor's note: Victorian novelists were much less reticent, perhaps because also less conscious, in introducing eroticism into their children's books. There is a great deal of what we should now recognize as overt eroticism in the writings of Elizabeth Wetherell (*The Wide Wide World*) and even more obviously in Florence Montgomery's novels published in the 1860s and 1870s which are about children and were read by children although the author disclaims in at least one preface that this was her intention.

emotional fixations of the other characters converge, undergoes a series of different and sometimes contradictory emotions, among them her affection for Monsieur de Nancé, her adoptive father; by the end of the tale, this feeling has become an obsession with all the ingredients of a true passion. Christine – neglected by her own parents – plays at having François as her brother – but she is overjoyed when she is adopted by François' father Monsieur de Nancé as a future fiancée for his son, transforming the make-believe brother into a real betrothed. Though, he is, in fact, a substitute fiancé because Christine, although she believes she will marry him, is really marrying Monsieur de Nancé himself; indeed her manifestations of tenderness and affection are all for the man who is for her a substitute for God.

... I am yours, for you made me, and I shall always be yours as I was when you received me from my parents. When will you come back, dear Father? When will I have the joy of embracing you and François? ...

As we can see, she had all but forgotten François! But such passages prove the infinite emotional potentialities of the children's novel.

In England, Florence Montgomery also wrote of passion. *Misunderstood*, her best-known book deals with the story of two young brothers whose mother has died some years before the story opens: the title refers to the elder, an apparently uncaring, extroverted child, constantly in mischief and leading his little, delicate, wistful brother into danger. The widowed father believes that Humphrey is totally careless and incapable of feeling, whereas in reality he cherishes a sense of irreparable mourning for his dead mother.

However, this sort of make-believe where everyone plays at being somebody else, acts the part of another, or reverses roles, abolishes the reality of familiar relationships so that the player wonders who are his true parents (those who brought him into the world or those for whom he feels) and inevitably leads to a loss of identity. In such novels – from Madame de Ségur's shrewdly observed stories to those of her crudest imitators – a whole technique of interchange and gradual merging can be detected; playmates become brother and sister, the stranger turns into the cherished son, or the elder sister takes the dead mother's place – the girl grows protective and the boy gentle and dependent so that the roles, with their attendant characteristics, are reversed. Characters play different parts and in doing so they change their skins, they change sex: girls are tomboys while boys are dreamy and sensitive; the only thing that matters is to exist for someone else, to have a comrade, to form a group or a couple. But something has to be forfeited and that is freedom, which is only possible to those who have experienced loneliness, for freedom consists in going beyond loneliness once a person has realized how unimportant he is to others and therefore how very much alone everybody really is. This is what Jean Vingtras desperately seeks and Gavroche actually experiences. Gavroche is, in fact, the only child-hero whom friendship passes by – for one cannot really consider as friendship his casual, fleeting relationship with the two little companions of a single night who vanish next day, swallowed up in the surge of the crowd while Gavroche is left on the pavement, indifferent, unresentful, alone and free.

Children dread such experiences, however. They have no desire for freedom, they like adventures to lead to its opposite: security. To enter wholeheartedly into the world of adventure – or that of the unknown – one must be able to forget temporarily one's immediate surroundings, forget, in fact, oneself, but children have to see what is going on all the time, what is round about them; they have to be aware of themselves. The realistic literature we have been discussing satisfies them precisely because it always brings them back to a world they can take in at a glance – back to themselves. So that, in the last analysis, such literature must be judged on the quality of awareness it offers.

It may be of some significance that the impact of the popular nineteenth-century writer – especially the great writer – was mainly visual. Victor Hugo, Dickens, Erckmann and Chatrian, all in their very different ways and on different levels, conjured up pictures. This tremendous stress on realistic vision is particularly attractive to children. A child's everyday home life plays so essential a part in his psychological balance and emotional security that for him the simple fact of naming familiar objects is a satisfaction – hence his tendency to count, collect and list. In this respect the masterpiece of realistic literature for children is assuredly the *Little House* series by Laura Ingalls Wilder, an untutored writer who might be seen as the Grandma Moses of fiction. The daughter of settlers turned farmers, she drew upon her store of childhood memories to write unsophisticated yet subtle books which are stories about things: Laura, her parents and her little sisters re-invent reality while accomplishing their daily tasks inside their diminutive home, stranded in the middle of the great Wisconsin forest, like an island in the ocean. Literary reminiscences play no part in her natural ability to observe each gesture with a little girl's inquisitive eyes, and when she offers her simple descriptions of hunting, preserving meat for the winter, bartering butter and weaving straw hats for protection against the sun, it is not in imitation of *Robinson Crusoe* but is an unconscious echo of the survival theme that was the subject of one of the greatest books of all time.

Here again Madame de Ségur excels, getting all she can out of the possibilities of the inventory. For there is no

question of her omitting a single item from a doll's ward-
robe. With Madame de Ségur the particular always over-
shadows the general, the proper noun the common noun:
not flowers, but carnations and mignonette grow in the
exemplary little girls' garden. Her partiality for detail is
undoubtedly a feminine trait; but then this is feminine
literature written for women, albeit small ones. Today, as
always, the realistic novel bears a feminine signature:
Colette Vivier, in France; Eve Garnett, Joyce Brisley and
Rumer Godden in Britain, Maria Gripe in Sweden, Johanna
Spyri in Switzerland and Liouba Voronkova in the U.S.S.R.
Though the characters in these books are very ordinary
children and not imaginary beings, the atmosphere is
strangely reminiscent of *Finn Family Moomintroll* and its
fantastic world.

All things considered, the over-awareness of detail
and the obsessive fear of missing a single item are really
more akin to surrealism than to fantasy. The reader, like
the writer, is imprisoned by his vision, immobilized by an
art which is neither musical nor melodic and which, ignor-
ing space and its continuity, only accumulates objects to
saturation point. The restricted setting – a house, a garden,
a village – is gradually filled with unimportant but necessary
objects, gestures and actions, and tea-time like Oblomov's[20]
morning, stretches and stretches till it is the size of a
book. At the end of one of Madame de Ségur's books
all those who have played a part in the story – however incidental this part may have been – are rounded
up and disposed of, so that there are no loose ends:
Marguerite marries Paul, Léon becomes a general, Jacques
a civil servant and Yolande Tourne-Boule an actress . . .
such endings offer no food for the imagination or open-
ings on to the future, it is simply a method of closing

20. *Oblomov* (1858), was a novel by Goncharov and a masterpiece of the
Russian 'realist' school.

down – yet another manifestation of the inventory technique. Everything is organized regardless of time and space. It is as if childhood, at the moment of vanishing, passes all its possessions in review for the last time.

Just as a little girl arranging her doll's house puts each little piece of furniture in its allotted place and all the different actors of static comedy in the positions they must occupy for evermore – the mother near the baby's cot, the father reading his paper and the cat by the fire – so Madame de Ségur organizes her doll's house at the end of each book. This is the only way a child has of conceiving his own future: a well organized home with everybody in his proper place and no room for chance – which is movement and danger – no room, in fact, for adventure.

8. *Adventure*

Many misconceptions about the nature and scope of children's books have arisen from the word 'adventure'. Judging from most of the titles of children's classics, it would seem that the adventure myth is as indispensable to them as it is to adults: Alice's adventures, Pinocchio's adventures, Tom Sawyer's adventures: there are surprising adventures, fantastic adventures, extraordinary adventures, marvellous adventures ... and one might assume that all children's stories are adventure stories because adventure is what they require, and what people like them to read. It is not even necessary to carry out a survey on children's literary tastes to discover, in fact, a notable discrepancy between the term 'adventure' and a child's conception of it[1] for a casual conversation with any child will give the same result: their idea of what distinguishes an adventure story is both vague and ambiguous. This idea will vary, of course, according to the child's sex, social background and age, but as a general rule one might say that for children an adventure story is any story which they have enjoyed enough to read from beginning to end. And after all, what could be more natural than this failure to agree on such a very complex matter? Children are quite right to see both *Les malheurs de*

1. See the inquiries carried out by 'La Joie par les livres' in *Bulletin d'analyses de livres pour enfants*, No. 12, June 1968 and by the *Bibliothèques pour tous de l'A.C.G.F.*: *Les Livres qu'ils aiment*, Ed. de l'Ecole 1966.

Sophie and *Treasure Island* as adventures; the outcome of every story involving action of any sort and told in such a way as to provoke a feeling of excitement can be seen as an adventure – depending on the susceptibility and the inclination of the reader. What happens to Sophie when she nibbles the candied fruit is an adventure as much as a 'misfortune', at least to the unsophisticated appreciation of a child. The more experienced reader, however, will, in fact, instinctively recognize *Le Tour du monde en quatre-vingts jours* or *Treasure Island* as adventure stories while excluding *les Malheurs de Sophie* and *Alice's Adventures in Wonderland* from this category.

The distinction is perhaps easier to grasp if we consider the problem from the point of view of the author rather than from that of the reader. For it is the greater or lesser distance from which an author perceives his hero which determines whether or not a story is an adventure story. It is really a question of the writer's being in control of the hero and making him do what he intends or, on the contrary, of his becoming so completely involved in his characters that it is they who act out the story. It is clear that when Lewis Carroll and Madame de Ségur conceived Alice and Sophie they were totally possessed by their respective heroines and that they subsequently had very little option in the matter of these young people's behaviour. However preposterous Sophie's ideas or apparently arbitrary Alice's vicissitudes these are always rooted in the unconscious; both Alice and Sophie are the product of their authors' forgotten frustrations, remorse and regrets. The odd and unexpected experiences of these two little girls are the more or less disguised and symbolic projections of Lewis Carroll's and Sophie de Ségur's desires and obsessions. They assert themselves but are constantly being trapped by their own actions, even though their actions are often inconclusive. The plurality of 'misfortunes' and 'adventures' is a mere concession to form – both heroines experience, in fact, just a single misfortune and a single adventure: Sophie, destruction and its aftermath of punishment; Alice, standing on a threshold which cannot be crossed. And only the ingeniousness of these two writers succeeds in making this repetitive, obsessional pattern so exciting that it always takes the reader by surprise.

The reader finds himself in a closed circle, however, where the author, involved with his hero, does not so much invent stories as transcribe one ever-recurring narrative that reflects and symbolizes his own past. Children's stories, because they are stories about children written by grown-ups, are predominantly nostalgic.

Another type of writer retains complete control of his hero and is sufficiently detached from him to organize each detail of his existence. In this case – that is, when the choice lies entirely with the author – he generally opts for adventure. The events in the story assume an air of fortuitousness and things seem to happen as they do in real life, where the future is in God's hands and no one is any the wiser. This type of writer is primarily a technician, a master craftsman, who can forget himself and control his memories; the adventure story is the product of a well-organized imagination; for, as Edgar Allen Poe, one of the pioneers of this art, said: 'Accidents must be the result of ceaseless, unerring calculation'.[2]

Unlike the writer intent on capturing the atmosphere of childhood, where time stands still, frozen in the eternity of make-believe, and each day brings further proof of the fact that the child is a child forever:

> We were, fair queen,
> Two lads that thought there was no more behind

2. Quoted by Jules Verne in *Le Sphynx des glaces*, chapter 1.

> But such a day tomorrow as today
> and to be boy eternal.3

the adventure-story writer – whose main task is to reproduce the continuity of existence – willingly submits his tale to the passage of time. Here the impression of reality and life is not the result of occasional realistic details or meticulously drawn settings and props; it is derived from the ceaseless, irresistible impetus of an adult existence where each day is different from the last. Consequently, one of the favourite forms adopted by these writers is autobiography. This is the form of *The Arabian Nights*, notably of 'Sinbad the Sailor', a story which has all the characteristics of the adventure story – and with a wealth of imagery! Autobiography – which according to Americo Castro is of Semitic origin – inspired the Arabian travellers' tales, then the picaresque novel, and from Spain passed into England. The first person singular has made adventure stories plausible from *Lazarillo de Tormes* to *Robinson Crusoe* and even to *Treasure Island*. For the 'I', far from internalizing the story, places it on the contrary squarely on the plane of the authentic tale and adds a further dimension, the satisfaction of both the story-teller and his audience: I who am talking to you, my friends, and whom you see before you, laden with years and with honour, I myself have lived these things . . .

This unfolding of a hero's life to the rhythm of a story led quite naturally to the concept of the journey, and adventure stories very soon became synonymous with travellers' tales. But there are journeys and journeys . . . the long, complicated journey abutting on the unknown, and the simple, straightforward return journey. *The Odyssey*, for instance is, according to Vladimir Jankélévitch, an example of the counterfeit adventure story:

3. Shakespeare, *The Winter's Tale*, I, ii, 62-5.

. . . the temptations of Ulysses are incitements to stay, not to move on: they are static rather than kinetic; the traveller is invited to interrupt his journey and to stop on the way, dawdle and drink in the shade. His temptresses represent for the wanderer the pleasures of a sedentary life and a fixed abode. So that, in fact, it is the voice of duty which says to Ulysses: 'Arise! Set forth! Ever further!' Yet even duty does not suggest that further must be boundless . . . There is only one thing Ulysses desires and that is to get back home, back to his faithful wife Penelope, to his house in Ithaca and the smoke of his little village. He never sought adventure. Indeed, this pseudo traveller is only an adventurer by necessity; basically he is a stay-at-home, and his peregrinations, from this point of view, turn out to be rather tame adventures.[4]

Whereas 'Sinbad the Sailor' is the story of a quest for adventure: Sinbad is the adventurer of adventurers, a man who cannot stay in one place and for whom departure is a vocation. He leaves without reason or objective, but because an irresistible impulse hurls him across the seas, to adventures that are as arbitrary as their motivation.

With *Robinson Crusoe* adventure and adventurer acquire a new depth through the interplay of two contradictory aspects of the journey: the thirst for the unknown and the yearning for the familiar. Here the adventure enriches the individual by compelling him towards action and resourcefulness. Like Sinbad, Robinson Crusoe is involved in his adventures by accident, but he is immediately in control, setting mishaps aright, resisting temptations and re-creating a familiar world where he can settle down and take root. This is a return to safety and to a time not by chance, but by the regular rhythm of work and where there is no place for the unexpected.

Adventure stories stem from one or the other of these three interpretations of the journey: that of Ulysses, of

4. Vladimir Jankélévitch, *L'Aventure, l'ennui, le serieux*, Aubier, Paris, 1963

Sinbad or of Robinson Crusoe, together with their respective imagery, accessories and symbolism. This attempt at
defining the general outline of such a literature may make
it appear most inappropriate for children, despite the
antiquity of travel and quest myths and the universal theme
of danger. Furthermore, the adventure was not incorporated
into European tales until a relatively late date. It is only
quite recently, with Edgar Allen Poe and Robert Louis
Stevenson, that the story-teller became aware of his role as
manipulator of accidents and began to use them with the
calculated intention of a chess player working out his moves.

A reader must possess a certain degree of detachment
and experience before he can put himself entirely in the
hands of the narrator; and consequently it is rather the
adolescent than the child who reads the great adventure
stories from 'Sinbad the Sailor' and *The Odyssey* to *Treasure
Island*, *Huckleberry Finn*, *Kim*, Dumas' novels, Erckmann
and Chatrian's epics and even the inventions of Jules
Verne and his imitators. There is also a purely practical
and mechanical reason for this, which is that adventures
tend to be long; pages and pages of preparation are required
by some authors while they set the scene before they can
suddenly emerge taking the reader by surprise at the most
unexpected moment. Naturally enough, adventure stories
really came into their own with serialization.

It is adults, not children, who have the patience to follow
a serial from one issue to the next. Younger children see
books as concrete objects, things complete in themselves
to be read at one sitting – even if they are re-read later on.
Thus the fragmentation of a serial story is alien to a young
child's concept of reading and to his natural impetuosity.
Furthermore, adventure stories are frightening. Of course
children enjoy being thrilled and will enjoy a frightening
story so long as it presents some kind of distancing effect –
a transposition of reality – and does not seem 'true'. Indeed,

Red Riding Hood's wolf or the denizens of Wonderland –
even Madame de Ségur's poor *Ourson* – might be more
terrifying than the pirates of *Treasure Island* if they were
considered as real. But whereas the monstrous projections
of the unconscious express a basic necessity and truly represent incomprehensible evil powers from which there is no
escape, the villains in Stevenson's story are specifically
contrived in order to produce fear.

In so far as they are wilfully created by the author's
conscious mind – subtle as this mind might be and however
successful its artistry – they produce only the impression of
fear because they lack the ambiguity of symbols. The
actions of such characters must inevitably be directed
towards evil; they steal, murder and betray their fellows
when and how they please; furthermore they threaten the
hero's physical self – hence that of the reader – and not his
unconscious – something not to be discounted. When the
scarred old captain arrives at the 'Admiral Benbow' followed later by Black Dog, Jim Hawkins certainly does not
feel pleasantly excited! Nor does he, when he discovers the
conspiracy on the high seas, feel anything but intense,
overpowering terror. In reading these novels, the reader
becomes acquainted with anxiety in all its forms. A certain
pleasure can be derived, for instance, from sensations of
disquiet or depression, or such sensations can be warded
off by translating them into the disturbing or grotesque
representations of dreamland and fairy tales, but there is
nothing in the least pleasurable in knowing that a mutinous
sailor stands at your back ready to plant a dagger between
your shoulder blades. *Treasure Island* can have a terrifying
effect on children if they read it when they are too young,
and the terror it inspires is not enjoyable.

In the same way, though for totally different reasons,
children – and indeed many adults – cannot bear to read
the last pages of *Vicomte de Bragelonne* where the musketeers

meet their respective deaths. Little by little as we grow older we witness the deaths of many of the greatest and most moving characters in fiction – Prince Andrei, Clélia Conti etc. – but such heartbreaking separations are akin to those encountered in real life, and the violent, complex emotions they provoke are of a different order from those aroused in a child by the irrevocable disappearance of d'Artagnan and his companions which spells the terrible finality of the story's ending. We can cope – to a greater or lesser degree – with life's ordeals, but we cannot give up the world of pure adventure once it has been experienced even for a brief space – once we have become involved in the imaginary, possible (for everything is possible here) yet ideal existence of characters who are like us in every respect – except perhaps in their breathing apparatus; for they live on pure oxygen and tread the path of destiny with perfect ease at a speed which accelerates with every page ... The only remedy for such losses (and one which is widely adopted) is to re-read over and over again the first two volumes: *Les trois Mousquetaires* and *Vingt ans après*.

It now becomes easier to understand why children are not quite in their element in real adventure stories and why such stories are better suited to adults – although only adults who have retained the enthusiasm of youth. The adventure-story writer usually treats ideas casually and is not particularly aware of the workings of his unconscious neither is he susceptible to anxiety. Alexandre Dumas is a perfect example of these qualities. His wonderful stories are unadulterated narrative with no further implications. The hurdles in his heroes' path are not symbols of their creator's obsessions, for Dumas has no obsessions – only the one *idée fixe* of keeping his story going; his curiosity enables him to invent what will happen next and why, and how the hero will leap into the saddle and ride away. The obstacles his fertile imagination piles up are devices to maintain the pull of his narrative, and for this purpose nothing is too trivial, conventional – or, indeed, improbable. Dumas does not even exploit mystery; on the contrary, he takes the reader into his confidence from the very beginning, making him his accomplice and his equal and giving him the satisfaction of being in the know – almost of inventing the story himself. This literature is, indeed, full of satisfactions. These are achieved by combining the two essential conditions of adventure story-telling: the free use of invention together with the disciplined rejection of everything which does not have a purely narrative purpose.

We have already observed the essentially symbolic character of all really important children's stories from the folk tale on. All children's writers have other considerations than the purely artistic; even Hans Andersen who was very much aware of the possibilities of his medium and intensely pre-occupied with the manner of telling a story, sometimes found his narrative slipping away from him; his lucidity consisted mainly in the organization and handling of images and emotions. Children recognize and find themselves only in stories written by men and women who are still involved in their own childhood; men and women who would, perhaps, be incapable of contemplating the future were they not able to transform past experience into art.

Dumas' books, on the other hand, satisfy a maturer concept of literature which children can and should acquire at about twelve years of age. They correspond to a whole change of attitude – the discarding of childish egocentricity and guardedness for more outward-looking satisfactions. Dumas' reader must be sufficiently independent not to be influenced by conventional opinions and he must have learnt how to read without expecting to derive pleasure from the literary style. Alexandre Dumas has nothing to

offer on this level which is probably why he is hardly considered a writer and enjoys no literary reputation. He
remains a popular writer and therefore despised; no useful
information can be gleaned from his works, especially not
historical information for in this field his assertions are
highly questionable, neither are his works conducive to
reflection. Even the detective-story reader is considered
more highbrow than addicts of cloak-and-dagger stories,
for a good mystery is supposed to exercise the brain and
Dumas' books do not. In fact all that Dumas requires of
his readers is the ability to enjoy what is illogical and to take
pleasure in the pleasure of others – to let themselves be
carried away by somebody else's fantasies. Only a truly
adult mind is able to acknowledge personality as it deserves
or is capable of unbiased admiration.

As a matter of fact, children's literature has retained only
three things from the adventure story: a setting, a plot and
a character. The setting is an unbounded landscape – a
virgin forest or, more often, the American prairie or the
sea. The plot is that of Robinson Crusoe, and the character
is the outlaw. Fenimore Cooper was the first to make use
of the setting in his novels, and it was he too who introduced into literature the myth of the Far West and the Red
Indian. Strangely enough, Cooper's influence was greatest
on European novelists; Balzac and Eugène Sue transferred
the activities of his pioneers, trackers and hunters from
their wild, limitless background to the carefully partitioned,
circumscribed and suffocating environment of the great
city. After Cooper, the Western was only to find its full
expression on the screen.

However, the most popular children's books about Red
Indians appear, curiously enough, to have been written
mainly by Germans – Karl May and Fritz Steuber – or by
Frenchmen – Lucien Biart, Gustave Aimard and Gabriel
Ferry. Nowadays, however, the topic has lost much of its

charm, though mention should be made of stories set in the Pampas where, instead of being a cowboy as in the Western, the hero is a gaucho. Probably for reasons of economy this variant has never been taken over by the cinema and though it includes some remarkable works – notably *Martin Fierro* – it is not popular with children.

As to the Robinson Crusoe theme, it has been exploited mainly by educationalists, from Wyss's Swiss Family Robinson (1812) on. The image of the successful desert-islander is perhaps responsible for all the den-building, or simple picnicking incidents to be found in children's books. However, the theme has become domesticated and even in an adventure story it represents a breathing-space, a secure haven.

Then we have the hero as outlaw or superman. Such a character either opposes social conventions like Robin Hood or Tarzan or, more frequently, adopts the outlaw's disguise to defend established order and justice more freely. Tintin and all the youthful heroes of children's detective stories answer this last description. But the Robin-Hood or outlaw figure is a lonely figure and as such is not wholly acceptable to children. Alfred Assolant's Captain Corcoran has a tigress, Louison, as his faithful companion and Tarzan establishes a kind of society in the jungle, employing animal slaves and finally getting married, while today's young supermen are all surrounded by subordinates who set off their unique qualities of flair, adventurousness and daring. Such stereotyping inevitably detracts from the poetry of adventure. More than in any other form of children's literature the tendency to scale down has reduced the adventure story for children to a parody of the original. The proof, if proof is needed, can be found in those widely-read collections for older children and adolescents, where each volume is a more or less overt adaptation of some time-honoured adventure story such as *Moby Dick* or the novels of Jules Verne. These publications have not even the advantage of being unpretentiously entertaining: unless the author redeems his lack of inventiveness by the liveliness of his style, such products are at best only escapist reading.

Perhaps the most interesting, if not the most important interpretation of the adventure story is the 'anti-adventure'. Here the author makes a group of imaginative children – who are usually on holiday or in some other relatively independent situation – enact a make-believe of the conventional adventure. The game, however, suddenly becomes a reality when, by pure accident (a storm, a sprained ankle, the loss of a picnic basket or of a compass) a real adventure overtakes them. Arthur Ransome in his *Swallows and Amazons* books was a master of this art; one of his books bears the significant title: *We didn't want to go to sea.* The reaction against adventure stories can also be less ambiguous and more aggressive. Readers can be very suspicious of fantasy: you can't tell *me* stories, says the sensible, practical citizen. No, people don't always like to be told stories. Comfortably settled in an easy-chair with a book or a television set before them, they dread being taken in by some 'tall story'. Children's books sometimes borrow classic adventure-story motifs in order to burlesque them: a typical example is *Baron Munchäusen*, but there are many others, especially in comics. As a matter of fact, ludicrous adventure is the basic theme of the two most popular French comic strips: *La famille Fenouillard* and *Le Savant Cosinus* by Christophe. The most unexpected and pleasing instance of negative adventure is *Babar's Travels*, a picture book for very young children, by Jean de Brunhoff, which employs all the clichés of genre: shipwreck, desert-island, cannibals, capture, escape and, finally, war. These adventures experienced by two elephants, Babar and his wife Céleste, are translated into the context of the animal tale for the under-five-year-old with its totally different conventions. By choosing this unexpected setting for his story, the author has, in a sense, defused the adventures and undermined their ritual.

There is another type of adventure story, the detective novel, still to consider. This is also an unconscious expression of the anti-adventure. In fact, such detective stories for children as those popularized in the series *Club des cinq, Alice detective, Fantomette, Michel detective* etc., are not *real* detective stories at all, if this definition implies a synthesis of mystery and power of deduction, as Boileau and Narcejac5 assert: a good detective is one who relies to an equal extent on art and method. In children's versions, however, the mystery is dispelled from the very beginning and the combination of poor atmosphere and paltry crime make them unexciting reading. Of course, what is really missing here is death, the essential ingredient of any detective novel. The presence of the corpse – which does not necessarily involve violence – is the one indispensable piece of data in the problem; without it, the mystery is reduced to a guessing game at about the level of a crossword.

Some riddles, however, are cleverer than others but those with which the children's detective is confronted are, at best, silly and usually non-existent; the criminal is unmasked in the first chapter and the quest becomes a simple pursuit in which the reader is on the pursuer's side and so experiences neither suspense nor anguish; this is no adventure. This form of literature is a reversion to the most elementary form of compensatory tale.

If it were not for Jules Verne there would be little to say in favour of children's adventure stories. Children definitely enjoy this great writer's stories but did he really write for so restricted a public? Where, in fact, really is his readership? The answer is that Jules Verne set out to write

5. *Le Roman policier*, Petite bibliothèque, Payot, 1964.

scientific novels for schoolboys and that in France, at any rate, grown-ups have ignored him until quite recently. Unlike Robert Louis Stevenson, Jules Verne was no artist. He never seems to have worried about organizing his vast imaginative material to its best advantage; surprise is no part of his repertoire, and the dreams he inspires come only later, to reveal his power; in fact, he seems to have been scarcely aware of his gifts. Although Jules Verne was justified in acknowledging Dumas as his master, he was not, like Dumas, brilliant at reconstructing history, the world and society. Dumas did what he pleased with his raw material without worrying about ideas, facts or even the promptings of his own memory. Jules Verne was the exact opposite: he had no artistic aims or theories but was absorbed in his memories and obsessions like all great writers who speak a language children can understand. Yet he opted to express himself through the adventure story – a form requiring a total understanding of one's gifts – and for his muse he chose the machine which definitely directed his tales towards the future. According to Hetzel, *Voyages extraordinaires* was originally intended as an educative work:

... his published works together with those in preparation will form a whole corresponding to a project the author defined when he subtitled his series *Voyages dans les Mondes connus et inconnus*. His aim, in fact, is to give a brief outline of all the geographical, geological, geophysical and astronomical knowledge modern science has achieved and – with his customary skill – to write a new history of the Universe.[6]

Although Jules Verne was probably unaware of the fact, this project was an aesthetic one; Edgar Allen Poe describes it as a means of acquiring a new territory for imaginative expression by turning science into a subject for poetry.

6. Hetzel's preface to *Aventures du Capitaine Hatteras*.

The first step was a mere gesture – introducing numbers into a fictional narrative. In *De la Terre à la lune*, one of the earlier *Voyages extraordinaires*, the story moves through an absolute forest of numbers: statistics, measurements and calculus affect the reader hypnotically while satisfying a childish liking for precision and competition.

Figures, moreover, are reassuring: they appear to confine the narrative's boundless extravagance, within reasonable limits; they constitute a barrier against the unknown. Jules Verne unobtrusively switches from the number-figure to the code-figure as he exploits the possibilities of language such as word play. Indeed, many of his novels are based on a coded message and its systematic decoding.[7] His endless scientific descriptions are incredibly boring attempts to prove what cannot be proved and children tend to skip them, but in spite of this they are soothing. The excitement of the hero's imminent departure when the invention that will change him into a superman is about to be put to the test, contains a frightening challenge to reality: the flying machine which transports the engineer Robur up into the clouds, to the terror of the world, or the disaster which precipitates Cyrus Smith and his companions on to the mysterious island may obliterate reality for a time, but not for long; the intrepid explorer will have to contend with its undiminished powers only too soon. It is as though the further he rises into space the more firm land draws him back; as in that lovely story by Ray Bradbury where the cosmonauts, having successfully landed on Venus, are overcome by rain and boredom and wander over the newly conquered planet dreaming only of the 'rest-station' where easy chairs, coca-cola and the last 'tube' to Earth await them.

7. The significance of figures in the *Voyages extraordinaires* has been very shrewdly discussed by Marcel Moré in *Le très curieux Jules Verne*, Gallimard, 1960.

In trying to create a further – therefore impossible world – Jules Verne never quite succeeds in getting his feet off the ever-present ground. He always just fails to make his extraordinary mechanisms real. Mechanical inventions, the conquest of space and the domination of nature are not sufficient in themselves to make a different universe, mainly because both nature and mechanical devices resist total domination: Professor Lidenbrock never attains the centre of the earth and Captain Hatteras is overcome by 'polar madness' when he reaches the North Pole. The exact point at which man will overstep the laws of nature and enter the realm of the unknown is always just out of reach; although imagination and daring thrive and increase at every new obstacle, it is all to no avail. Only in his madness can Captain Hatteras achieve his conquest of the North Pole. Ultimate discovery, power or happiness cannot be experienced on earth; the only hope is to get as far from earth and as near to the unattainable as possible – and then, like Robinson Crusoe, recreate a familiar, practical, sheltered world. Jules Verne first establishes entirely abnormal conditions of existence and then reassembles all the disjointed elements of normal life in a sort of jigsaw. There is, for instance, an astounding variety of improbable houses, all larger than life, and equipped – like Des Esseintes' house[8] – with all the comforts civilization can produce: 'Snow House';[9] the cabin of the Nautilus;[10] the roof-house in 'L'Albatross',[11] 'Granite House'[12] and all the rolling or floating houses – *La Maison à Vapeur*, *La Jangada* etc. There is only one 'journey' where we do not find ourselves confronted at the very heart of the most fantastic adventure with domestic life at its cosiest, and that is the expedition

8. J.-K. Huysman, *A rebours* (1884).
9. *Les Aventures du Capitaine Hatteras*.
10. *Vingt mille Lieues sous la mer*.
11. *Robur le conquérant*.
12. *L'Ile mystérieuse*.

5*

to the surrealist splendours at the centre of the earth, undertaken by Professor Lidenbrock and his nephew Axel. Here Jules Verne seems to have almost entirely surmounted the attractions home-comings usually exert, but in every other novel he adds a new and poetic dimension to the original Robinson Crusoe theme. Incapable of achieving the unknown, his heroes make the best of a bad job by forming an alliance with nature or merging with their machines or with the elements: they become creatures of the air, like Robur, of the abyss, like Lidenbrock, of the sea, like Nemo, or of snow and ice, like Hatteras, while still remaining children of the earth and of civilization. The scientist settlers of *L'Ile mystérieuse* might well be seen as anti-Tarzans, inhabitants of a mechanized world rather than explorers participating in the natural life of the savage.

Jules Verne did not always make the journey's end and the contrivances of the voyage his main concern. He sometimes showed the adventure as a mere personal whim and not as something essential to man's soul: the better to master it, he made it the subject of a bet. Characters make wagers concerning their fate and the author takes up the gamble of telling an impossible tale. Thus the adventures in *Les tribulations d'un Chinois en Chine*, *Le Tour du monde en quatre-vingts jours* (*Round the World in Eighty Days*) and *Le Testament d'un excentrique* – absurd from sheer excess of organization – are all sparked off by a wager. Or he can ward off the terrifying consequences of scientific inventions by taking them to the limits of absurdity as in *Une Fantaisie du Dr Ox*. In this way, having led the reader right up to the frontiers of fantasy, Jules Verne dispels the mirage either by introducing reality in its more practical details, or by adopting a tone of mocking humour, which may account for the fact that his books are never frightening and rarely even disturbing – unless this feature is due simply to a rather crude style and a

certain clumsiness in the story-telling. There is a definite
split between Jules Verne's fertile imagination and his
ability to express it: even a commonplace science fiction
story can be more disquieting than his stories, not to
mention those great visionaries Poe, Lovecraft, Kafka
or Kubin, though the worlds to which they introduce us
are not, in the end, any more ghastly than those created
by Jules Verne. His books are definitely for the fifteen-
year-old, except for those stories where the adventure is
social instead of individual, where the hero opposes other
men rather than nature, and exploits science to achieve
power like Hector Schultze[13] or Harry Killer[14] and not
like Hatteras or Lidenbrock, to satisfy an obsessive desire
for regression. Harry Killer is the founder of the artificial
city of 'Blackland' situated in the heart of Africa and
uncharted by any official map; its inhabitants 'excluding
children, are six-thousand-eight-hundred strong', they
are divided into 'merry fellows', 'civil body' and 'slaves',
each group occupying a reserved district. In the exact
centre of the city stand two towers: one houses the tyrant,
the other 'the factory'. Everything is scientifically conceived in this strange locality: the surrounding lands
have been reclaimed and irrigated; the factory supplies
the town with water and electricity; hygienic amenities
are provided for all citizens alike and each inhabitant
possesses a telephone; the factory produces 'flying machines'
and missiles. The 'slaves' are cruelly treated and worked
to death by the 'merry fellows' while the 'civil body'
serves the double purpose of police force and army and
lives in the expectation of becoming eventually 'merry
fellows'. There is, naturally, no possibility of escape,
for Blackland is surrounded by a magnetic zone where
all who venture are instantly electrocuted. This ill-fated

13. *Les 500 Millions de la Begum.*
14. *L'étonante Aventure de la mission Bersac.*

city based on crime and thriving on crime – prophetic
compound of order and disorder, of technicality and
savagery – vanishes in a terrible conflagration amidst
the howling of mutinous slaves. In his last and least-
known work, Jules Verne really surpassed himself;
from the simplest ingredients he has achieved a world
which resembles nothing else and is terrifying in its
otherness.

9. *Childhood Regained*

Jules Verne's inspired books, so often dismissed by critics, illustrate very clearly the difficulty of defining what is meant by children's literature. People are generally unwilling to recognize the value of works they cannot classify and are suspicious of books which do not correspond to any of the headings in their aesthetic catalogue – books which are 'badly written' have no psychological complexity, do not deal with human relationships and eroticism, or any of the essential material of the novel. They do not know what to make of stories where metaphysical torment and anguish are translated into childish images and symbols. They cannot absolutely place the books in any respectable category but can only lump them together under some general heading like 'detective novels', cloak-and-dagger adventures, science fiction, books for children ... thus banning them entirely from the realm of 'literature'.

They are sometimes obliged, however, to admit that one of these books has a unique charm and poetry. In such cases they explain away the paradox by setting up a complex system of references and comparisons: Hans Andersen is a more sober exponent of German romanticism; Lewis Carroll is a precursor of surrealism; Madame de Ségur is an interesting example of sadism; and as for Jules Verne, well, he is a sort of prophet who foretold the exploits of Charcot and later, Gargarin and Borman and predicted jet-propulsion –

and some people go so far as to mention him in the same breath as Lautréamont.

Nonetheless, the fact remains that such literature is considered a by-product. It is acknowledged so far and no further, confined to all intents and purposes to the transitory 'initiation' function. Initiation to what? Why, literature, of course! For there is such a thing as 'great' literature in the same way as there is 'great' music – and children's literature is evidently not of this kind.

It should by now be clear that since what is known as 'literature' does not and never did, in fact, exist, it is absurd to imagine that any sort of initiation can be required; that the emotions we experience through reading develop by stages, each stage represented by the various examinations leading from primary school to university entrance, and that an understanding of what we read can only be acquired the hard way through a succession of school essays and literary comprehensions. Children's literature is not a temporary substitute for something which the novice in a great, mystical scheme for the gradual achievement of transcendental knowledge is not yet ready to tackle. Critics – always ready to distribute either good or bad marks – are prepared to judge this 'by-product' by academic standards and to declare that one of its productions is or is not 'literature', is or is not 'well-written', and that it stands or does not stand a chance of becoming a 'classic'.

Scholastic disputes of this order only disguise the truth, which is that such works exist in their own right and not as rungs on the ladder to adult reading or that of middle-class citizens reared on the humanities. To say that a book is a 'first step' or that an author is an 'initiator' is to subscribe to a preposterous belief in a formidable staircase negotiated easily by some – who take it merrily two steps at a time – while others puff and plod or simply settle down contentedly on the first flight. Such assertions imply a difference in the quality of emotions experienced by children and adults, and indicate an attempt to put a value even on sensibility.

If, however, we cease to think in terms of initiation and consider the problem as a matter of experience, it is clear that a person who reads *Babar* for the first time experiences something just as singular and absorbing as he who reads for the first time *The Brothers Karamazov*. What is important in the case of children's literature is not whether or not it is literature, but that it should be for children; its interest and significance depend on this specific characteristic. Of course, the world of childhood can be interpreted – and misinterpreted – in many ways. A writer may find the idea of describing a child's behaviour as attractive and as entrancing as that of describing the vicissitudes of a bankrupt businessman, for instance, or of a butcher, or a left-wing journalist etc. – and he will have no more difficulty in doing so if he is Dickens (who did just that) or Balzac (who had planned to do it). But a child-hero is not essential to the definition of a children's book – indeed many of the best books for children have no such hero, as we have frequently observed. What is required of children's literature is that it should evoke the world of childhood. But to what extent does it succeed in doing so to the satisfaction of children and of adults or of a given society?

It can be said that there are no rules and very few practical restrictions. Books for children are not books for grown-ups on a reduced scale; indeed, they can be long and tedious, like those by Jules Verne, or dry and difficult like the 350 pages without illustrations of *King Mathias I* by Janusz Korczak – whose popularity proves that children also need to think of the world in political terms.

Of course there is no question of underestimating the all-important problem of learning to read – but this is outside the scope of our essay and belongs almost more to sociology than to education. Learning to read is frequently given too much importance and tends to confuse the issue. It is very far from being the whole problem – in fact it is merely peripheral. It is true that certain mental blocks resulting from a child's innate linguistic disability may easily cause him to reject the written word, but most difficulties can be overcome, and what the bright child reads at the age of eight will be read by the average child a couple of years later. The working-class child's greater emotional maturity enables him to experience pleasure and excitement with greater intensity; and he may be drawn by his instinctive curiosity to read and appreciate works that might be considered too advanced for his age and understanding. The fact that there are these discrepancies should not deter us from the main consideration, that of feeling, and its true relation to childhood. There are enchanted moments in literature, not only in children's books, which are accessible to every child: Saint Francis of Assisi begging his 'little sisters the swallows' to be silent because the noise of their chirping drowns his voice when he is preaching, or that inspired passage that describes the child Tolstoy's awakening, so full of charm, irony and tenderness that nothing but the language of childhood itself could express it naturally and faithfully. This does not, of course, mean that children will automatically enjoy Franciscan poetry or Tolstoy's novels, but only that such memorable passages are essential to a genuine literature for children.

In addition to the passage quoted earlier are such as Cyrus Smith's encounter with Captain Nemo in the underground grotto;[1] the death of Joli-Coeur the monkey;[2] Mowgli dancing and brandishing the 'red flower'[3] or the relentless litany of the destruction of Sophie's doll:

1. Jules Verne, *L'Ile mystérieuse*.
2. Hector Malot, *Sans Famille*.
3. Rudyard Kipling, *The Jungle Book.*

> Sophie sobbed, but the doll was no less pale ... Sophie
> sobbed, but the doll was no less bald.[4]

and many others. These are only my own selection; they
cannot take account of other people's favourites – little
white pebbles that reappear at random, emerging from the
unconscious by a quirk of memory and which vary according
to the person's own experience of life.

Why have certain writers chosen this particular medium
to express tragedy, comedy or mystery? This is a question
no one – perhaps not even the writers themselves – can
answer accurately. We must be content with examining
their work and with suggesting that Madame de Ségur and
Hans Andersen and Jules Verne and Lewis Carroll were all
anomalies, 'literary cases' but are not all poets and makers
of imaginary worlds 'cases'? It can be said with some
measure of certainty that what really adulterates children's
literature, deprives it of its individuality, degrades and
destroys it, are preconceptions or stereotyped images; for
instance, the notion that children are all innocence and its
opposite that they are entirely perverse beings. Though
these two visions of childhood are as different in character
as they are in significance, they have both played an important part in poetic representations of children. The first
has not perhaps been very influential in literature, but it has
been extremely popular in other forms of art. Related as it is
to the cult of the child Jesus in Roman Catholic countries,
it may account for the relatively small number of books
for children to be found in Spain and Italy. Moreover, in
the Latin countries, children are notably absent from
sixteenth-, seventeenth- and eighteenth-century adult literature as well as from that of the first half of the nineteenth
century. But in the plastic arts representations of childhood
abound, as is shown by the way angels are transformed

4. Madame de Ségur, *Les malheurs de Sophie*.

into soft, rounded little cherubs in an idealized, stylized rendering of childhood, a rendering that literature also preferred.

The concept of childish perversity depends much less on superficial motivations; it is not so abstruse and is, indeed, based to a certain extent on observation. As a truism it has always had its place in popular saws; but, especially since the relevations of psychoanalysis, it has acquired a much wider acknowledgement. Fiction is, of course, the perfect medium in which to portray ambiguities and contrast outward innocence with psychological depravity. Thus an enigmatic little animal has brought its ambiguity to literature. This emphasis on the mysteries of childhood partly explains childhood, but it is infinitely more satisfying to adult rather than childish curiosity. It establishes a dialogue between the grown-up and the child he has been, or thinks he has been, or would have liked to have been, or believes children to be. None of this is proper to a literature for children, who, in fact, do not need such interpretations. It is the books where the problems of childhood play no part that appeal to them most strongly and make them realize who they are and of what they are capable; whereas the slightest attempt at explaining childish attitudes and reactions detracts from the specifically childish character of the story and turns it into something else. Only the greatest masters have succeeded in achieving this duality of purpose; perhaps Hans Andersen is the only one to have done so entirely, for he was so completely in control of his own mastery that he could take the risk of exploring and revealing a world complex and subtle enough to intrigue and move the adult reader, without ever changing his tone or breaking the spell which held his natural unsophisticated audience.

Children's literature has nothing whatsoever to lose by insisting on its own individuality. On the contrary, this will only point up the artificiality of conceiving 'literature' in terms of social value only. Why indeed should a certain form of artistic expression be judged superior to another, considered to be the only one worthy of being called 'literature', and established as the norm, when all that really counts is that human expression should have the widest possible range, no matter from where it springs or what form it adopts? What is important is man's ability to create, to give shape to the imaginary. However, classifications, conventional values and academic strictures are more easily broken nowadays. The impulse that helped us to explore primitive art should likewise enable us to understand that oral literatures, nursery rhymes and folk tales have as much significance as any other form of artistic expression and that these also contain the unexpected revelation that can lead to the moment of grace. And this is the way children's literature should be approached.

Of course, though primitive art is created by primitives, children's books are not written by children, and that there is a conscious intention in writing for children may provoke a certain resistance. The Bantu had no thought or knowledge of Picasso when they conceived their masks and sculptures; they merely reproduced their own image as they perceived it, and there were only a few artists among the Bantu who were capable of such invention. This sort of discussion can only lead to paradox and absurd formulations such as that no one but an adventurer can write adventure stories, a peasant, folk tales or a simpleton paint 'naïve paintings'.

Writers can hark back to their childhood – as, indeed we all do – but to them the answering voice speaks with sufficient clarity to form words, sentences, stories . . . a voice of such authenticity and limpidity as to be recognized by children themselves, by every child . . . And from this collaboration of the listening artist and the distant childhood voice a poem emerges:

Piping down the valleys wild,
Piping songs of pleasant glee,
On a cloud I saw a child,
And he laughing said to me:

'Pipe a song about a lamb!'
So I piped with a merry chear.
'Piper, pipe that song again,'
So I piped: he wept to hear.

'Drop thy pipe, thy happy pipe:
Sing thy songs of happy chear;'
So I sung the same again
While he wept with joy to hear.

'Piper, sit thee down and write
In a book, that all may read'
So he vanish'd from my sight,
And I pluck'd a hollow reed.

And I made a rural pen,
And I stain'd the water clear,
And I wrote my happy songs
Every child may joy to hear.5

In our present state of passivity towards social pressures, such voices offer each of us protection and a means of finding ourselves. Indifference and blind acceptance on our part is unpardonable because it increases the general confusion, obstructs our resistance to the pressure to conform. Flimsy, pretentious novels, abridged versions of famous works, the ceaseless reprinting of children's 'classics' and the nauseating exploitation of the most lifeless plots and the most repetitive techniques, all help in the moral and social conditioning of children today – and of middle-class children no less than the others. How can they defend

5. William Blake, *Songs of Innocence and Experience*, Introduction.

themselves unaided against the pretences and forgeries which assail them from all sides? Yet even more than many adults, children are susceptible to the excitement of discovering a new and liberating voice.

Appendix

The Will-o'-the-Wisp is in the Town *by Hans Andersen*

There was a man who once knew many stories, but they had slipped away from him – so he said; the Story that used to visit him of its own accord no longer came and knocked at his door: and why did it come no longer? It is true enough that for days and years the man had not thought of it, had not expected it to come and knock; and if he had expected it, it would certainly not have come; for without there was war, and within was the care and sorrow that war brings with it.

The stork and the swallows came back from their long journey, for they thought of no danger; and, behold, when they arrived, the nest was burnt, the habitations of men were burnt, the hedges were all in disorder, and everything seemed gone, and the enemy's horses were stamping in the old graves. Those were hard, gloomy times, but they came to an end.

And now they were past and gone, so people said; and yet no story came and knocked at the door, or gave any tidings of its presence.

'I suppose it must be dead, or gone away with many other things,' said the man.

But the story never dies. And more than a whole year went by, and he longed – oh, so very much! – for the story.

'I wonder if the story will ever come back again, and knock?'

And he remembered it so well in all the various forms in which it had come to him, sometimes young and charming, like spring itself, sometimes as a beautiful maiden, with a wreath of thyme in her hair, and a beechen branch in her hand, and with eyes that gleamed like deep woodland lakes in the bright sunshine.

Sometimes it had come to him in the guise of a pedlar, and had opened its box and let silver ribbon come fluttering out, with verses and inscriptions of old remembrances.

But it was most charming of all when it came as an old grandmother, with silvery hair, and such large sensible eyes; she knew so well how to tell about the oldest times, long before the Princesses span with the golden spindles, and the dragons lay outside the castle, guarding them. She told with such an air of truth that black spots danced before the eyes of all who heard her, and the floor became black with human blood; terrible to see and to hear, and yet so entertaining, because such a long time had passed since it all happened.

'Will it ever knock at my door again?' said the man; and he gazed at the door, so that black spots came before his eyes and upon the floor; he did not know if it was blood, or mourning crape from the dark heavy days.

And as he sat thus, the thought came upon him, whether the story might not have hidden itself, like the Princess in the old tale? And he would now go in search of it; if he found it, it would beam in new splendour, lovelier than ever.

'Who knows? Perhaps it has hidden itself in the straw that balances on the margin of the well. Carefully, carefully! Perhaps it lies hidden in a certain flower – that flower in one of the great books on the book-shelf.'

And the man went and opened one of the newest books, to gain information on this point; but there was no flower to be found. There he read about Holger Danske; and the man read that the tale had been invented and put together by a monk in France, that it was a romance, 'translated into Danish and printed in that language'; that Holger Danske had never really lived, and consequently could never come again, as we have sung, and have been so glad to believe. And William Tell was treated just like Holger Danske. These were all only myths – nothing on which we could depend; and yet it is all written in a very learned book.

'Well, I shall believe what I believe!' said the man; 'there grows no plantain where no foot has trod.'

And he closed the book and put it back in its place, and went to the fresh flowers at the window; perhaps the story might have hidden itself in the red tulips, with the golden yellow edges, or in the fresh rose, or in the beaming camellia. The sunshine lay among the flowers, but no story.

The flowers which had been here in the dark troublous time had been much more beautiful; but they had been cut off, one after another, to be woven into wreaths and placed in coffins, and the flag had waved over them! Perhaps the story had been buried with the flowers; but then the flowers would have known of it, and the coffin would have heard it, and every little blade of grass that shot forth would have told of it. The story never dies.

Perhaps it has been here once, and has knocked – but who had eyes or ears for it in those times? People looked darkly, gloomily, and almost angrily at the sunshine of spring, at the twittering birds, and all the cheerful green; the tongue could not even bear the old, merry, popular songs, and they were laid in the coffin with so much that our heart held dear. The story may have knocked without obtaining a hearing; there was none to bid it welcome, and so it may have gone away.

'I will go forth and seek it! Out in the country! out in the wood! and on the open sea beach!'

Out in the country lies an old manor house, with red walls, pointed gables, and a red flag that floats on the tower. The nightingale sings among the finely fringed beech-leaves, looking at the blooming apple trees of the garden, and thinking that they bear roses. Here the bees are mightily busy in the summer-time, and hover round their queen with their humming song. The autumn has much to tell of the wild chase, of the leaves of the trees, and of the races of men that are passing away together. The wild swans sing at Christmas-time on the open water, while in the old hall the guests by the fire-side gladly listen to songs and to old legends.

Down into the old part of the garden, where the great avenue of wild chestnut trees lures the wanderer to tread its shades, went the man who was in search of the story; for here the wind had once murmured something to him of 'Waldemar Daa and his Daughters'. The Dryad in the tree, who was the story-mother herself, had here told him the 'Dream of the old Oak Tree'. Here, in the time of the ancestral mother, had stood clipped hedges, but now only ferns and stinging-nettles grew there, hiding the scattered fragments of old sculptured figures; the moss is growing in their eyes, but they can see as well as ever, which was more than the man could do who was in search of the story, for he could not find it. Where could it be?

The crows flew past him by hundreds across the old trees, and screemed, 'Krah! da! – Krah! da!'

And he went out of the garden, and over the grass-plot of the yard, into the alder grove; there stood a little six-sided house, with a poultry-yard and a duck-yard. In the middle of the room sat the old woman, who had the management of the whole, and who knew accurately about every egg that was laid, and about every chicken that could creep out of an egg. But she was not the story of which the man was in search; that she could attest with a Christian certificate of baptism and of vaccination that lay in her drawer.

Without, not far from the house, is a hill covered with red-thorn and broom; here lies an old gravestone, which was brought here many years ago from the churchyard of the provincial town, a remembrance of one of the most honoured councillors of the place; his wife and his five daughters, all with folded hands and stiff ruffs, stand round him. One could look at them so long, that it had an effect upon the thoughts, and these reacted upon the stones, as if they were telling of old times; at least it had been so with the man who was in search of the story.

As he came nearer, he noticed a living butterfly sitting on the forehead of the sculptured councillor. The butterfly flapped its wings, and flew a little bit farther, and then returned fatigued to sit upon the grave-stone, as if to point out what grew there. Four-leaved shamrocks grew there; there were seven specimens close to each other. When fortune comes, it comes in a heap. He plucked the shamrocks, and put them in his pocket.

'Fortune is as good as red gold, but a new, charming story would be better still,' thought the man; but he could not find it here.

And the sun went down, round and large; the meadow was covered with vapour: the moor-woman was at her brewing.

It was evening; he stood alone in his room, and looked out upon the sea, over the meadow, over moor and coast. The moon shone bright, a mist was over the meadow, making it look like a great lake; and, indeed, it was once so, as the legend tells – and in the moonlight the eye realizes these myths.

Then the man thought of what he had been reading

in the town, that William Tell and Holger Danske never really lived, but yet live in popular story, like the lake yonder, a living evidence for such myths. Yes, Holger Danske will return again!

As he stood thus and thought, something beat quite strongly against the window. Was it a bird, a bat, or an owl? Those are not let in, even when they knock. The window flew open of itself, and an old woman looked in at the man.

'What's your pleasure?' said he. 'Who are you? You're looking in at the first floor window. Are you standing on a ladder?'

'You have a four-leaved shamrock in your pocket,' she replied. 'Indeed, you have seven, and one of them is a six-leaved one.'

'Who are you?' asked the man again.

'The moor-woman,' she replied. 'The moor-woman who brews. I was at it. The bung was in the cask, but one of the little moor-imps pulled it out in his mischief, and flung it up into the yard, where it beat against the window; and now the beer's running out of the cask, and that won't do good to anybody.'

'Pray tell me some more!' said the man.

'Yes, wait a little,' answered the moor-woman. 'I've something else to do just now.' And she was gone.

The man was going to shut the window, when the woman already stood before him again.

'Now it's done,' she said; 'but I shall have half the beer to brew over again tomorrow, if the weather is suitable. Well, what have you to ask me? I've come back, for I always keep my word, and you have seven four-leaved shamrocks in your pocket, and one of them is a six-leaved one. That inspires respect, for that's an order that grows beside the sandy way; but that every one does not find. What have you to ask me? Don't stand there like a ridiculous oaf, for I must go back again directly to my bung and my cask.'

And the man asked about the story, and inquired if the moor-woman had met it in her journeyings.

'By the big brewing-vat!' exclaimed the woman, 'haven't you got stories enough? I really believe that most people have enough of them. Here are other things to take notice of, other things to examine. Even the children have gone beyond that. Give the little boy a cigar, and the little girl a new crinoline; they like that much better. To listen to stories! No, indeed, there are more important things to be done here, and other things to notice!'

'What do you mean by that,' asked the man. 'and what do you know of the world? You don't see anything but frogs and Will-o'-the-Wisps!'

'Yes, beware of the Will-o'-the-Wisps,' said the moor-woman, 'for they're out – they're let loose – that's what we must talk about! Come to me in the moor, where my presence is necessary, and I will tell you all about it; but you must make haste, and come while your seven four-leaved shamrocks, of which one has six leaves, are still fresh, and the moon stands high!'

And the moor-woman was gone.

It struck twelve in the town, and before the last stroke had died away, the man was out in the yard, out in the garden, and stood in the meadow. The mist had vanished, and the moor-woman stopped her brewing.

'You've been a long time coming!' said the moor-woman. 'Witches get forward faster than men, and I'm glad that I belong to the witch folk!'

'What have you to say to me now?' asked the man. 'Is it anything about the story?'

'Can you never get beyond asking about that?' retorted the woman.

'Can you tell me anything about the poetry of the future?'
resumed the man.

'Don't get on your stilts,' said the crone, 'and I'll answer
you. You think of nothing but poetry, and only ask about
that Story, as if she were the lady of the whole troop.
She's the oldest of us all, but she takes precedence of the
youngest. I know her well. I've been young, too, and she's
no chicken now. I was once quite a pretty elf-maiden,
and have danced in my time with the others in the moonlight, and have heard the nightingale, and have gone into the
forest and met the story-maiden, who was always to be
found out there, running about. Sometimes she took up her
night's lodging in a half-blown tulip, or in a field flower;
sometimes she would slip into the church, and wrap
herself in the mourning crape that hung down from the
candles on the altar.'

'You are capitally well-informed,' said the man.

'I ought at least to know as much as you,' answered
the moor-woman. 'Stories and poetry – yes, they're like
two yards of the same piece of stuff: they can go and lie
down where they like, and one can brew all their prattle,
and have it all the better and cheaper. You shall have it
from me for nothing. I've a whole cupboard-full of poetry,
in bottles. It makes essences; and that's the best of it –
bitter and sweet herbs. I have everything that people
want of poetry, in bottles, so that I can put a little on my
handkerchief, on holidays, to smell.'

'Why, these are wonderful things that you're telling!' said
the man. 'You have poetry in bottles?'

'More than you can require,' said the woman. 'I suppose
you know the history of "the Girl who trod on the Loaf,
so that she might not soil her Shoes"? That has been
written, and printed too.'

'I told that story myself,' said the man.

'Yes, then you must know it; and you must know also

that the girl sank into the earth directly, to the moor-woman, just as Old Bogey's grandmother was paying her a morning visit to inspect the brewery. She saw the girl gliding down, and asked to have her as a remembrance of her visit, and got her too; while I received a present that's of no use to me – a travelling druggist's shop – a whole cupboard-full of poetry in bottles. Grandmother told me where the cupboard was to be placed, and there it's standing still. Just look! You've your seven four-leaved shamrocks in your pocket, one of which is a six-leaved one, and so you will be able to see it.'

And really in the midst of the moor lay something like a great knotted block of alder, and that was the old grandmother's cupboard. The moor-woman said that this was always open to her and to every one in the land, if they only knew where the cupboard stood. It could be opened either at the front or at the back, and at every side and corner – a perfect work of art, and yet only an old alder stump in appearance. The poets of all lands, and especially those of our own country, had been arranged here; the spirit of them had been extracted, refined, criticized and renovated, and then stored up in bottles. With what may be called great aptitude, if it was not genius, the grandmother had taken as it were the flavour of this and of that poet, and had added a little devilry, and then corked up the bottles for use during all future times.

'Pray let me see,' said the man.

'Yes, but there are more important things to hear,' replied the moor-woman.

'But now we are at the cupboard!' said the man. And he looked in. 'Here are bottles of all sizes. What is in this one? and what in that one yonder?'

'Here is what they call may-balm,' replied the woman: 'I have not tried it myself. But I have not yet told you the "more important" thing you were to hear. THE

WILL-O'-WISP'S IN THE TOWN! That's of much more consequence than poetry and stories. I ought, indeed, to hold my tongue; but there must be a necessity – a fate – a something that sticks in my throat, and that wants to come out. Take care, you mortals!'

'I don't understand a word of all this!' cried the man.

'Be kind enough to seat yourself on that cupboard,' she retorted, 'but take care you don't fall through and break the bottles – you know what's inside them. I must tell of the great event. It occurred no longer ago than the day before yesterday. It did not happen earlier. It has now three hundred and sixty-three days to run about. I suppose you know how many days there are in a year?'

And this is what the moor-woman told:

'There was a great commotion yesterday out here in the marsh! There was a christening feast! A little Will-o'-the-Wisp was born here – in fact, twelve of them were born all together; and they have permission, if they choose to use it, to go abroad among men, and to move about and command among them, just as if they were born mortals. That was a great event in the marsh, and accordingly all the Will-o'-the-Wisps, male and female, went dancing like little lights across the moor. There are some of them of the dog species, but those are not worth mentioning. I sat there on the cupboard, and had all the twelve little new-born Will-o'-the-Wisps upon my lap: they shone like glow-worms; they already began to hop, and increased in size every moment, so that before a quarter of an hour had elapsed, each of them looked just as large as his father or his uncle. Now it's an old established regulation and favour, that when the moon stands just as it did yesterday, and the wind blows just as it blew then, it is allowed and accorded to all Will-o'-the-Wisps – that is, to all those who are born at that minute of time – to become mortals, and individually to exert their power for the space of one year.

'The Will-o'-the-Wisp may run about in the country and through the world, if it is not afraid of falling into the sea, or of being blown out by a heavy storm. It can enter into a person, and speak for him, and make all the movements it pleases. The Will-o'-the-Wisp may take whatever form he likes, of man or woman, and can act in their spirit and in their disguise, in such a way that he can effect whatever he wishes to do. But he must manage, in the course of the year, to lead three hundred and sixty-five people into a bad way, and in a grand style, too; to lead them away from the right and the truth; and then he reaches the highest point. Such Will-o'-the-Wisps can attain to the honour of being a runner before the devil's state coach; and then he'll wear clothes of fiery yellow, and breathe forth flames out of his throat. That's enough to make a simple Will-o'-the-Wisp smack his lips. But there's some danger in this, and a great deal of work for a Will-o'-the-Wisp who aspires to play so distinguished a part. If the eyes of the man are opened to what he is, and if the man can then blow him away, it's all over with him, and he must come back into the marsh; or if, before the year is up, the Will-o'-the-Wisp is seized with a longing to see his family, and so returns to it and gives the matter up, it is over with him likewise, and he can no longer burn clear, and soon becomes extinguished, and cannot be lit up again; and when the year has elapsed, and he has not led three hundred and sixty-five people away from the truth and from all that is grand and noble, he is condemned to be imprisoned in decayed wood, and to lie glimmering there without being able to move; and that's the most terrible punishment that can be inflicted on a lively Will-o'-the-Wisp.

'Now, all this I know, and all this I told to the twelve little Will-o'-the-Wisps whom I had on my lap, and who seemed quite crazy with joy.

'I told them that the safest and the most convenient

6

course was to give up the honour, and do nothing at all; but the little flames would not agree to this, and already fancied themselves clad in fiery yellow clothes, breathing flames from their throats.

' "Stay with us," said some of the older ones.

' "Carry on your sport with mortals," said the others.

' "The mortals are drying up our meadows; they've taken to draining. What will our successors do?"

' "We want to flame; we will flame – flame!" cried the new-born Will-o'-the-Wisps.

'And thus the affair was settled.

'And now a ball was given, a minute long; it could not well be shorter. The little elf-maidens whirled round three times with the rest, that they might not appear proud, but they preferred dancing with one another.

'And now the sponsors' gifts were presented, and presents were thrown them. These presents flew like pebbles across the sea-water. Each of the elf-maidens gave a little piece of her veil.

' "Take that," they said, "and then you'll know the higher dance, the most difficult turns and twists – that is to say, if you should find them necessary. You'll know the proper deportment, and then you can show yourself in the very pick of society."

'The night raven taught each of the young Will-o'-the-Wisps to say, "Goo – goo – good," and to say it in the right place; and that's a great gift, which brings its own reward.

'The owl and the stork – but they said it was not worth mentioning, and so we won't mention it.

'*King Waldemar's wild chase* was just then rushing over the moor, and when the great lords heard of the festivities that were going on, they sent a couple of handsome dogs which hunt on the spoor of the wind, as a present; and these might carry two or three of the Will-o'-the-Wisps. A couple of old Alpas, spirits who occupy themselves with Alp-pressing, were also at the feast; and from these the young Will-o'-the-Wisps learned the art of slipping through every key-hole, as if the door stood open before them. These Alpas offered to carry the youngsters to the town, with which they were well acquainted. They usually rode through the atmosphere on their own back hair, which is fastened into a knot, for they love a hard seat; but now they sat sideways on the wild hunting dogs, took the young Will-o'-the-Wisps in their laps, who wanted to go into the town to mislead and entice mortals, and, whisk! away they were. Now, this is what happened last night. Today the Will-o'-the-Wisps are in the town, and have taken the matter in hand – but where and how? Ah, can you tell me that? Still, I've a lightning conductor in my great toe, and that will always tell me something.'

'Why, this is a complete story,' exclaimed the man.

'Yes, but it is only the beginning,' replied the woman. 'Can you tell me how the Will-o'-the-Wisps deport themselves, and how they behave? and in what shapes they have aforetime appeared and led people into crooked paths?'

'I believe,' replied the man, 'that one could tell quite a romance about the Will-o'-the-Wisps, in twelve parts; or, better still, one might make quite a popular play of them.'

'You might write that,' said the woman, 'but it's best let alone.'

'Yes, that's better and more agreeable,' the man replied, 'for then we shall escape from the newspapers, and not be tied up by them, which is just as uncomfortable as for a Will-o'-the-Wisp to lie in decaying wood, to have to gleam, and not be able to stir.'

'I don't care about it either way,' cried the woman. 'Let the rest write, those who can, and those who cannot likewise. I'll give you an old bung from my cask, that will open the cupboard where poetry's kept in bottles, and you may take from that whatever may be wanting. But you, my good man, seem to have blotted your hands sufficiently with ink, and to have come to that age of satiety, that you need not be running about every year for stories, especially as there are much more important things to be done. You must have understood what is going on?'

'The Will-o'-the-Wisp is in the town,' said the man. 'I've heard it, and I have understood it. But what do you think I ought to do? I should be thrashed if I were to go to the people and say, "Look, yonder goes a Will-o'-the-Wisp in his best clothes!"'

'They also go in undress,' replied the woman. 'The Will-o'-the-Wisp can assume all kinds of forms, and appear in every place. He goes into the church, but not for the sake of the service; and perhaps he may enter into one or other of the priests. He speaks in the Parliament, not for the benefit of the country, but only for himself. He's an artist with the colour-pot as well as in the theatre, but when he gets all the power into his own hands, then the pot's empty! I chatter and chatter, but it must come out, what's sticking in my throat, to the disadvantage of my own family. But I must now be the woman that will save a good many people. It is not done with my good will, or for the sake of a medal. I do the most insane things I possibly can, and then I tell a poet about it, and thus the whole town gets to know of it directly.'

'The town will not take that to heart,' observed the man; 'that will not disturb a single person; for they will all think I'm only telling them a story if I say, "The Will-o'-the-Wisp is in the town, says the moor-woman. Take care of yourselves!"'

List of Authors

AIMARD, Gustave (1818–85). French novelist, author of numerous adventure stories set in the Far West or at sea: *Les Trappeurs d'Arkansas*, *Belle-Franche*, *Les Chercheurs de pistes*, etc.

ALCOTT, Louisa May (1832–88). American author of books for girls: *Little Women* (1867–69) was the first of her books about the March sisters and she also wrote *Good Wives* (1869), *Little Men* (1871), *Eight Cousins* (1874), *Jack and Jill* (1880).

ANDERSEN, Hans Christian (1805–75). Danish author born at Odense. He was the son of a poor cobbler and enjoyed a happy childhood until his father died and his mother married again. He went to Copenhagen where he hoped to become first a dancer, then a singer; but, although these ambitions came to nothing, Jonas Collins, a theatrical manager, took an interest in this bright, almost illiterate adolescent, and obtained for him a grant which enabled him to attend school and then university. Andersen soon became a favourite among artists and in high society. He started to write poetry and prose poems, travelled in France, Spain and Italy and wrote a long novel: *Improvisatoren* (1835, tr. M. Howitt 1845). He formed a number of emotional friendships with very young girls amongst whom was the Swedish singer Jenny Lind. He was to write another novel, some travel stories and his autobiography (first in draft for his friends in 1832, published in Denmark as *Levnedsbogen*, 1926; then for publication in Germany in 1847 – *Das Märchen meines Lebens ohne Dichtung*, tr. M. Howitt. *The True Story of My Life*, 1847; and finally in 1855 *Mit Livs Eventyr*, tr. W. Glyn Jones,

The Fairy Tale of My Life, 1954). But his real genius revealed itself in fairy tales and it is for these that he will be remembered. After his first collection of tales was published in 1835 he brought out one every year at Christmas time.

ASBJORNSEN, Peter C. (1812–85) and MOE, Jörgen (1803–82). Norwegian naturalists and folklorists, authors of *Norwegian Folk Tales* (1861).

ASSOLANT, Alfred (1827–86). French novelist whose *Aventures merveilleuses mais authentiques du Capitaine Corcoran* mingle excitement with humour in the style of Jules Verne.

AULNOY, Madame d' (1650–1705). French short-story writer. Her *Contes de Fées* (1698) are mainly inspired from folk tales and include 'L'Oiseau bleu', 'La Chatte blanche', 'Finette Cendron' and 'Gracieuse et Percinet'.

AYMÉ, Marcel (1902–67). French novelist and playwright, author of stories for children: *Les Contes du chat perché* (1939).

BARBAULD, Anna Laetitia (1743–1825). English poet and essayist. She wrote three children's books: *Evenings at Home, Lessons for Children* and *Hymns in Prose for Children*.

BARRIE, James Matthew (1860–1937). English writer and playwright, author of *Peter Pan* (1904), *Peter Pan in Kensington Gardens* (1906) and *Peter and Wendy* (1911).

BARTO, Ania. Contemporary Soviet poetess born in 1906 who writes exclusively for children. Her first collection was published in 1925.

BASILE, Gianbatista (Gian Alesio Abattutis) (1575–1632). Italian writer who retold a number of popular tales, 'Puss in Boots', 'Cinderella' etc. His *Cunto de li Cunti* or *Pentamorone* (1634–6) is written in Neopolitan dialect and is full of burlesque metaphors.

BAUM, L. Frank (1856–1919). One of America's most famous children's writers. His series on 'the wonderful land of Oz' began with *The Wonderful Wizard of Oz* in 1900 and was continued after his death by various writers.

BERNA, Paul. Contemporary French children's author. His first book *Le Cheval sans tête* (1955) is also probably his best.

BERQUIN, Arnaud (1749–91). French writer, author of stories and playlets for children collected under the title *L'Ami des enfants* (1782–3).

BIANKI, Vitali. Contemporary Soviet writer specializing in books on nature and animals.

BIART, Lucien (1828–97). French novelist. Published some adventure stories for children in the *Magasin d'éducation et de récréation: Monsieur Pinson, Lucia Avila, Les Aventures d'un jeune naturaliste au Mexique, Le Pensativo, La Vallée des colibris*.

BLYTON, Enid (1900–1968). One of the most prolific of children's writers, translated into almost every European language. The 'Five' books, a mystery series, are among her best-known works.

BONSELS, Waldemar. Contemporary German children's writer, author of *Die Biene Maja* (Maja the Bee), and *Mario, ein Leben im Walde* (Mario, a Woodland Story).

BOSCO, Henri. Contemporary French novelist born in 1888. He has written for children: *L'Âne culotte, L'Enfant et la rivière, Le Renard dans l'île, Barjabot*.

BOSTON, Lucy. Contemporary English writer. Her series of books for children, *Green Knowe*, was awarded the Carnegie Medal in 1961.

BOURLIAGUET, Léonce (1895–1965). French children's writer, author of *Contes de mon Père Le Jars* (1944) and *Quatre au cours moyen* which was awarded the Prix Jeunesse for 1934.

'BRENDA' (Mrs Castle Smith). A nineteenth-century children's writer whose best-known novel *Froggy's Little Brother* (1875) describes the appalling conditions in which slum children lived in those days.

BRENTANO, Clemens (1778–1842). German writer. In collaboration with Achim von Arnim he published *Des Knaben*

Wunderhorn (1806) (The Youth's Marvellous Horn), a collection of folk songs which inspired the Brothers Grimm. His *Kinder-märchen* (Children's Tales) and *Rheinmärchen* (1838) (Tales from the Rhine) are adaptations of folk tales.

BRISLEY, Joyce L. Contemporary English author of a very popular series of girls stories: *Milly-Molly-Mandy Stories* (1928).

BROOKS, Leslie. English illustrator of nursery rhymes: *Ring O' Roses* (1922) and *Johnny Crow's Garden* (1935).

BROWN, Margaret Wise. Contemporary American short-story writer for very young children.

BRUNHOFF, Jean de (1899–1937). Creator of Babar. The first album: *Aventures de Babar, le petit éléphant* (1931) was followed by five others.

BRUNHOFF, Laurent de. Jean de Brunhoff's son has continued his father's series. His first book, *Babar and that Rascal Arthur*, was followed by several others.

'BRUNO' (Madame Fouillé). The wife of a philosopher whose children's stories *Francinet* (1870) and *Le Tour de France de deux enfants* (1886) were secular classics throughout the period of the Third Republic.

BRYANT, Sara Cone. American pedagogue and writer, author of *How to Tell Stories to Children* (1911).

BUCKERIDGE, Anthony. Contemporary English writer for children, author of *Jennings at School*, etc.

BURNETT, Frances Hodgson (1849–1924). Writer of children's stories, born in Manchester, emigrated to the U.S.A. in her youth. Best known as the author of *Little Lord Fauntleroy* and *The Secret Garden*.

BURROUGHS, Edgar Rice (1875–1950). American writer, author of the Tarzan series. His first book *Tarzan of the Apes* (1912) has inspired a number of films and comic strips.

BUSCH, Wilhelm (1832–1908). A German cartoonist who created two frightful little boys, Max and Moritz.

BUZZATI, Dino (1906–72). Italian novelist. He has written a couple of whimsical stories for children: *Barnabo delle montagne* (1933) (Barnabus in the Mountains) and *Il segreto del bosco vecchio* (1935) (The Secret of the Old Wood) which may also be read as moralities for grown-ups and *La famosa invasione degli orsi in Sicilia* (1958) (When Bears invaded Sicily).

CALDECOTT, Randolph (1846–86). English illustrator of nursery rhymes, tales and folk songs.

CAPUTO, Natha (1904–67). French educationist, writer and critic of children's literature. Besides her many translations of children's books she is the author of a collection of stories for young children: *Contes des quatre vents* (1956).

CARROLL, Lewis (Charles Lutwidge Dodgson) (1832–98). English writer of mathematical treatises and children's books. The son of a clergyman and eldest of a large family, he used to entertain his brothers and sisters with his stories and rhymes when he was still only a boy. Educated at Rugby and Christ Church, Oxford, he was lecturer in mathematics at Oxford from 1855 to 1888. His mathematical works were written under his real name, but he signed his books for children Lewis Carroll. These were written for his little friends – all little girls – with whom he corresponded regularly. His hobby was photography, and his favourite subjects were, again, little girls. His masterpieces are *Alice's Adventures in Wonderland* (1865), *Through the Looking Glass* (1872) and *The Hunting of the Snark* (1876), a long poem.

CASSIL, Leo. Contemporary Soviet novelist born in 1905, who writes mainly for children. One of his best novels is *Chwambranie* (1933).

CENDRARS, Blaise (Frédéric Sauser) (1887–1961). Swiss writer and a great traveller who collected and adapted for children an anthology of African folk tales: *Petits Contes nègres pour les enfants de blancs.*

CHAVEAU, Léopold. Contemporary French writer and illustrator of children's books. His best work, *Histoire du petit Père Renaud* (1932) is out of print.

CHRISTOPHE (Georges Colomb) (1856–1945). Science master and one of the creators of the comic strip. *La Famille Fenouillard* (1889), *Le Sapeur Camembert* (1890), *Le Savant Cosinus* (1893).

COLLODI (Carlo Lorenzini) (1826–90). Italian journalist and translator of Perrault's fairy stories who became famous as the author of *Pinocchio, storia di un burattino,* which was published in *Giornale per i bambini* (The Children's Magazine) in 1881. Collodi's story was made into a cartoon film by Walt Disney.

COMASSI, Mario. Contemporary Italian writer for children, author of *Spinarella.*

COMENIUS (Jan Amos Komensky) (1592–1670). Czech educationalist and writer. He became a priest of the Church of the Bohemian Brethren and worked as a teacher. He left Czechoslovakia in 1621 and worked abroad where he was known all over Europe for his educational theories. Author of *Didactica magna* (1640), *Orbis Pictus* (1657).

COOPER, James Fenimore (1798–1851). Famous American adventure-story writer, author of *The Last of the Mohicans* (1826).

CROMPTON, Richmal. English authoress of the famous 'William' series about the escapades of a grubby and mischievous schoolboy and his gang of friends. There are almost forty 'William' titles which have been translated into many different languages.

DAY, Thomas (1748–89). British author of the *History of Sandford and Merton* (1783–9), in which he tried to reconcile Rousseau's naturalism with a sounder morality.

DE AMICIS, Edmondo (1846–1908). Italian journalist and writer, author of *Cuore* (1886) (tr. G. S. Godkin, *Heart,* 1895; S. Jewett, *The Heart of a Boy,* New York, 1960).

DELETAILLE, Albertine. Contemporary Belgian illustrator and writer, author of a number of *Père Castor* albums.

DEULIN, Charles (1827–77). French writer and folklorist, author of *Contes d'un buveur de bière* (1868) and *Contes du Roi Gambrinus* (1874), inspired from Flemish folk tales.

DODGE, Mary Mapes (1831–1905). Her children's novel, *Hans Brinker or the Silver Skates*, enjoyed world-wide success. She had a decisive effect on children's literature in the U.S.A. as the founder of a children's magazine, *St Nicholas*, which she edited until her death.

ERCHOV. Contemporary and friend of Pushkin's. Author of *Konyok-gorbunok*, a verse story inspired from an old Russian legend and which has become a Russian children's classic.

ERCKMANN, Emile (1822–99) – CHATRIAN, Alexandre (1826–90). French writers who wrote in collaboration a collection of *Romans Nationaux populaires*.

FARRAR, Frederick William (1831–1903). Professor at Trinity College, Cambridge and the author of school stories that were famous in their day and to which Kipling often refers with nostalgic irony. *Eric or Little by Little* was published in 1858 and *St Winifred's or the World of School* in 1862.

FAUCHER, Paul (1898–1967). French pedagogue and creator of the *Père Castor* albums. Under his direction a team of writers, psychologists, folklorists and illustrators, produced nearly 350 albums grouped under various titles: *Albums-jeux, Roman des bêtes, Enfants de la terre, Montreur d'images*. His son, François Faucher, has succeeded him and continues in his father's footsteps. These albums are published by Flammarion.

FAUCONNIER, Geneviève. Contemporary French writer, author of the children's books *Trois petits enfants bleus* (1936).

FERRY, Gabriel (1809–52). French writer of adventure stories, author of *Le Coureur des bois, Costal l'Indien, Scènes de la vie sauvage*, written between 1840 and 1850.

FIELDING, Sarah (1710–68). Sister of Henry Fielding and author of one of the first books for girls: *The Governess or the Little Female Academy* (1765).

FOREST, Antonia. Contemporary English writer, author of the children's book *Peter's Room* (1961).

GAMARRA, Pierre. Contemporary French writer mainly of books for children: *Le Mystère de la berlurette* (1957), *Le Trésor de tricoire*, etc.

GARNER, Alan. Contemporary English author of some notable stories of magic and fantasy: *The Moon of Gomrath* (1963), *The Weirdstone of Brisingamen* (1960) and *Elidor* (1965).

GARNETT, Eve. Contemporary English writer and illustrator. One of her children's books, *The Family from One End Street* (1937), where she describes the circumstances of a working-class family, was taken up by socialists in their campaign for the clearance of city slums.

GENLIS, Madame de (1746–1830). French educationalist, author of edifying books for children: *Adèle et Théodore* (1782), *Les Veillées du château* (1784).

GIPSON, Fred. Contemporary American writer of animal stories, author of *Old Yeller*.

GODDEN, Rumer. Contemporary English writer, author of a number of children's books: *The Doll's House, Holly and Ivy*, etc.

GOSCINNY, René. Contemporary French humorist, author of comic strips and a schoolboy series: *Le petit Nicolas* (1954) with illustrations by Sempé.

GRAHAME, Kenneth (1859–1932). English writer whose most famous work is *The Wind in the Willows* (1908).

GREENAWAY, Kate (1846–1901). Famous and prolific English illustrator of children's books.

GRIMM, Jacob (1785–1863) and Wilhelm (1786–1859). Authors of works on German philology and German folklore, and especially of the famous collection of fairy tales *Kinder- und Hausmärchen* (1812–13) first translated into English in 1823 under the title *German Popular Stories* with illustrations by Cruikshank.

GUILLOT, René (1900–1969). French children's writer: his book *Sama, Prince des éléphants*, was awarded the Prix Jeunesse for 1950. He was awarded the International Hans Christian Andersen Prize in 1964.

HALE, Katherine. Contemporary Scottish author and illustrator of the delightful 'Orlando the Marmalade Cat' series.

HALE, Lucretia (1820–1900). American nineteenth-century writer, author of the *Peterkin Papers* (1886) published in the magazine *Young Folks*.

HARRIS, Joel Chandler (1848–1908). American author of the famous *Uncle Remus* stories which first appeared in the magazine *Atlanta Constitution*. In these stories Harris shows a remarkable knowledge of Negro folklore and Negro dialect.

HENTY, George Alfred (1832–1902). English author of over a hundred carefully researched and exciting historical adventure stories. Many of his stories featured some celebrated naval or military commander and had titles such as *Under Drake's Flag*, *With Wolfe in Canada*, *With Clive in India* and *With Buller in Natal*.

HETZEL, Pierre-Jules (1814–86). French writer and publisher. In 1864 he founded, with Jean Macé, *Le Magasin d'éducation et de récréation* which appeared once a fortnight until 1915. Under the pen-name of P. J. Stahl he translated and adapted for children a number of foreign works and wrote story-books for very young children: *Aventures de Madame Lili*, etc. and novels for older children: *Histoire d'un âne et de deux jeunes filles*, etc.

HOFFMANN, Heinrich (1806–94). A German artist and writer whose masterpiece, *Struwwelpeter* (1845) is, with *Max und Moritz*, one of the great German humorous classics.

HUGHES, Thomas (1822–96). English writer of the first school story, *Tom Brown's Schooldays* (1857), in which he depicted, with didactic purpose, schoolboy cruelties and loyalties.

JANSSON, Tove. Contemporary Finnish writer and illustrator of children's books born in 1914. Miss Jansson writes in Swedish and is the author of *Moomins* (tr. Elizabeth Portch *Finn Family Moomintroll*, 1961) and a number of other books, for which she was awarded the Nils Holgersson Prize in 1953 and the International Hans Christian Andersen Prize in 1966.

JARRELL, Randall (1914–65). American poet and critic, author of *Animal Family* (1965), a book for children.

JOHNS, Captain William Earl (1893–1968). English author of the flying series that features the famous 'Biggles'. Between 1935 and the early 1950s Johns published over seventy 'Biggles' books.

KÄSTNER, Eric. German writer born in 1899. His most famous children's book is *Emil und die Detektive* (1929, tr. E. Hall *Emil and the Detectives*, 1960) and he was awarded the International Hans Christian Andersen Prize for 1960.

KINGSLEY, Charles (1819–75). English author who wrote two fine adventure stories, *Westward Ho!* (1855) and *The Heroes* (1856), as well as his most famous book, *The Water Babies* (1863).

KIPLING, Rudyard (1865–1936). English novelist and author of many children's books, among which the most famous are *The Jungle Book* (1894), *Just So Stories*, *Puck of Pook's Hill*, *Stalky & Co.*

KNIGHT, Eric (1897–1943). An English journalist and novelist who emigrated to America. His best-selling children's book was *Lassie, Come Home* (1940). It was a phenomenal success and was made into a film.

KORCZAK, Janusz (1878–1940). Polish doctor and educationalist. He believed that children should be given freedom and a sense of responsibility, and he was a pioneer of 'children's republics'. He died in the concentration camp of Treblinka where he had chosen to accompany the two hundred little Jewish inmates of the children's home of which he was head. He is the author of *King Matthias I* (1928).

KRUSS, James. Contemporary German writer of children's stories and poems born in 1926. He was awarded the International Hans Christian Andersen Prize in 1968 for his important contribution to children's literature, which includes *Der Leuchtturm auf dem Hummerklippen* (1956), *Die glücklichen Inseln hinter dem Winde* (1958) and *Mein Urgrossvater und Ich* (1959).

KULLMANN, Harry. Contemporary Swedish writer of children's books, born in 1919. He was awarded the Nils Holgersson Prize in 1955 for *Hemlig resa*.

LAGERLOF, Selma (1885–1940). Swedish novelist and short-story writer, author of *Nils Holgerssons underbara resa* (1906–7) (*Nils Holgersson's Wonderful Journey*) a book for children commissioned by the Primary School Board for the teaching of national geography in which her description of a flight on gooseback delighted children of all countries.

LANG, Andrew (1844–1912). A professor and learned essayist whose continuing fame rests on the collections of fairy stories for children which he published between 1889 and 1913. *The Blue Fairy Book*, the first, was immediately successful and was followed by twenty-four other volumes. Lang's versions are among the best for children, containing a mixture of traditional stories, folk tales, fantasy, jingles and poetry.

LA ROCHE, Mazo de. Contemporary Canadian novelist, author of *The Explorers of the Dawn*, a book for children.

LEAR, Edward (1812–88). An artist and author of *The Book of Nonsense* (1846).

L'ENGLE, Madeleine. Contemporary American writer. Her best-known children's book is *A Wrinkle in Time* (1962).

LENSKI, Lois. Contemporary American writer of children's books describing everyday life in the different states, among which *Judy's Journey* (1943) is the most successful.

LEPRINCE DE BEAUMONT, Jeanne-Marie (1711–80). French writer and educationalist. Of her many books, *Le Magasin des enfants* (1757) which includes 'La Belle et la bête' is the best remembered.

LEWIS, Clive Staples (1898–1963). Professor of English at

Oxford and at Cambridge, specializing in medieval and Renaissance literature. He began to publish children's books in 1950. The last of the seven *Narnia* novels was awarded the Carnegie Medal.

LOBATO, Monteiro (1882–1948). One of Brazil's outstanding public figures, he founded the Brazilian publishing industry which had previously depended entirely on Portugal. In 1921 he began to write for children and, in his many books, uses fantasy and symbolism to describe social problems in Brazil.

LOFTING, Hugh (1886–1947). English artist and children's writer who created Dr Dolittle. The first of the series, *The Story of Dr Dolittle*, was published in 1920.

LONDON, Jack (1876–1916). American novelist who began life as an ordinary sailor, author of *The Call of the Wild* (1903) and the even more famous *White Fang*; both have a dog as hero.

MACÉ, Jean (1815–96). Founder of the Ligue de l'Enseignement and co-founder with Hetzel of *Le Magasin d'éducation et de récréation*. Author of children's stories *Les Contes du petit chateau* (1862), and a number of educational works: *Histoire d'une bouchée de pain* (1861), *Les Serviteurs de l'estomac* (1866) etc.

MAETERLINCK, Maurice (1862–1949). Belgian poet and dramatist, author of *L'Oiseau bleu* (1908, tr. A. T. de Mattos *The Blue Bird*, 1909) an allegorical play for children.

MALOT, Hector (1830–1907). French writer mainly remembered for his two books for children: *Sans famille* (1878) and *En famille* (1893).

MARRYAT, Frederick (1792–1848). English author who joined the Royal Navy at the age of fourteen and wrote some fine sea-adventure stories, among them *Mr Midshipman Easy* (1836) and *Masterman Ready* (1841). Probably his most popular book is *The Children of the New Forest* (1847).

MATUTE, Ana-Maria. Contemporary Spanish novelist born in 1926, author of *Paulina, el mundo y las estrellas* (1960) (Pauline, the World and the Stars).

MAURIAC, François (1885–1970). French novelist, author of *Le Drôle* (1933), a book for children.

MAY, Karl (1842–1912). German adventure-story writer, author of *Winnetou* (1892). This was the first of his Westerns, for which he is principally remembered.

MAYNE, William. Contemporary English writer of children's books. He was awarded the Carnegie Medal for *A Grass Rope* (1957).

MILNE, A. A. (1882–1956). Author of stories and verse for children: *Winnie the Pooh* (1926), *The House at Pooh Corner* (1928), *When We Were Very Young* etc.

MILOSZ, Oscar-Vladimir de Lubicz (1877–1939). Lithuanian poet who wrote in French. His book for children *Les Contes lithuaniens de ma Mère l'Oye* (1933) is inspired from his own national folklore.

MOLESWORTH, Mary-Louisa (1839–1921). Prolific writer of children's books. Her stories are rather conventional but not without charm as fantasies: *The Cuckoo-Clock* (1877), *The Tapestry Room* (1879) etc.

MOLNÁR, Ferenc (1878–1952). Hungarian playwright and novelist, author of *A Pál Utcai Fiúk* (1927, tr. L. Rittenberg, *The Paul Street Boys*, 1927) which touchingly captures the beauty and torment of youth.

MONESTIER, Marianne. Contemporary French journalist and author of children's books, of which *La petite fille de nulle part* (1961) is perhaps the most representative.

MUSÄUS, Johann-Karl-August (1735–87). German writer who was responsible for one of the first anthologies of folk tales: *Volksmärchen der Deutschen* (1782–87) (*German Folktales*).

NESBIT, Edith (1858–1924). English journalist and writer, socialist and member of the Fabian Society. The great charm of her children's books is probably due to the perfect balance she always maintains between fantasy and realism: *Five Children and It* (1902), *The Phoenix and the Carpet* (1904), *The Story of the Treasure-Seekers* etc.

NEVILLE, Emily. Contemporary American writer of children's books, author of *It's like this, Cat* which was awarded the Newbery Prize.

NEWBERY, John (1713–67). An English publisher who virtually created both children's publishing and children's bookshops in Britain. His shop near St Paul's Cathedral, 'The Bible and the Sun', stocked only children's books and was the outlet for his own publications. His first, *A Little Pretty Pocket Book* (1744) was both cheap (6d.) and well produced. In 1755 he brought out *Goody Two-Shoes* and its success encouraged him to abandon didactic literature. As the father of children's literature, he is remembered in America by the Newbery Prize, awarded annually for the best children's book.

NIGREMONT, Georges (Lea Pelletier) (1885–1971). A teacher and children's writer whose *Jeantou, maçon creusois* (1937) was awarded the Prix Jeunesse. Her books deal with everyday life either nowadays or in history and include *Les étranges voyageurs* (1949), *Le Prisonnier des Brages* (1954), *Quatre coups espacés* (1958), *La Ville déchirée* (1970).

NORTON, Mary. Contemporary English writer of children's books, author of *The Borrowers* which was awarded the Carnegie Medal in 1953.

O'HARA, Mary. American children's novelist who writes about horses and children. Her best-known books are *Thunderhead, My Friend Flicka*, and *Green Grass of Wyoming*.

ORWELL, George (1903–50). English writer, author of the satiric fantasy *Animal Farm* (1943), sometimes seen as a children's book.

PANOVA, Vera. Soviet novelist and short-story writer born in 1905. Though *Seryozhe* was written for adults most children will understand and appreciate this beautiful story.

PEARCE, Philippa. Contemporary English children's writer, author of *Tom's Midnight Garden* which received the Carnegie Medal in 1958, *A Dog So Small* etc.

PERRAULT, Charles (1628–1703). French writer, member of a distinguished bourgeois family of doctors, architects and intellectuals; he held various important administrative positions under Colbert before entering the Académie française in 1671, where he championed 'the moderns' against Boileau and wrote *Le Siècle de Louis le Grand* (1687) and *Le Parallèle des Anciens et des Modernes* (1688–97), which express his theories. Today he is mainly remembered for his re-telling of French folk tales, first in verse: *Grisélidis, avec le conte de Peau d'Ane et celui des souhaits ridicules* (1694), and then in a prose style of great beauty and simplicity: *Histoires et contes du temps passé avec des moralités* (1697), also known as *Contes de ma Mère l'Oye.*

PORTER, Eleanor H. American early twentieth-century writer whose edifying novel *Pollyanna* still enjoys a wide popularity in the U.S.A.

POTTER, Beatrix (1866–1943). English writer and illustrator of children's books, author of *Peter Rabbit* (1902), *Jemima Puddleduck, Mrs Tiggy-Winkle* and many others.

PREUSSLER, Otfried. Contemporary German writer of children's books, author of *Die Kleine Hexe* (1957) (*The Little Witch*).

RANSOME, Arthur (1884–1967). Author of *Swallows and Amazons* (1931) and many other books about the same children.

REED, Talbot Baines (1852–93). English author of a series of famous public-school stories, among them *The Fifth Form at St Dominics* (1881) and *The Cock House at Fellsgarth* (1890).

RENARD, Jules (1864–1910). French novelist and dramatist, author of *Poil de carotte* (1894, tr. G. W. Stonier *Carrots*, 1946) the story of an unhappy childhood which is sometimes seen as a children's book.

ROUSSEAU, Jean-Jacques (1712–78). Swiss-French writer and moralist, author of *Émile* (1762, tr. B. Foxly, 1930).

SAINT-EXUPÉRY, Antione de (1900–44). French novelist, author of *Le petit prince* (1943, tr. K. Woods *The Little Prince*, 1944), a fairy tale.

SALTEN, Felix. Contemporary German-Swiss writer, author of *Bambi* (1926), much popularized by Walt Disney's film of that name.

SANDBURG, Carl (1878–1967). American poet who wrote a collection of stories for children, *The Rootabaga Stories* (1922).

SCHMIDT, Annie. Contemporary Dutch writer of children's books, author of *Wiplala* (1957).

SÉGUR, Countess Sophie de (1799–1874). French writer of Russian extraction, daughter of Count Rostopschin, who was minister to the Tsar Paul I, but emigrated to France in 1717. After a rather unhappy marriage, she began writing at the age of fifty-eight for her grandchildren. Her first work *Nouveaux contes de fées* (1857) was followed by more than twenty novels for children, published by Hachette in the *Bibliothèque rose*.

SENDAK, Maurice. Contemporary American illustrator and writer whose sense of humour, feeling and technique have greatly influenced modern picture books. His books include *Where the Wild Things Are* and *The Night Kitchen*. In 1968 he was awarded the Hans Andersen Prize.

SETON, Ernest Thompson (1860–1946). American writer, author of *Wild Animals I have known* (1898) and one of the first to describe animals in their natural setting.

SEWELL, Anna (1820–78). English writer whose only book, *Black Beauty* (1877), the story of a horse, is considered by some to be the finest book ever written about an animal.

STRAPAROLA, Gianfrancesco (*c.* 1480–*c.* 1557). Italian short-story writer, author of *Le piacevoli notti* (1550–53) (*Joyous Nights*).

STEVENSON, Robert Louis (1850–94). Most of his books were written for children. *Treasure Island* (1887), published, as were the others, in the magazine *Young Folks*, is undoubtedly the most popular and could stand as a model for the adventure story. His volume of poetry for children, *A Child's Garden of Verses*, was published in 1885.

STOWE, Harriet Beecher (1811–96). American authoress known almost entirely for the classic work, *Uncle Tom's Cabin*.

SUTCLIFF, Rosemary. Contemporary English writer, justly famous for such books as *The Eagle of the Ninth*, *The Lantern Bearers* and *The Dragon Slayer*.

TOLKIEN, J. R. R. Contemporary English writer born in 1892, author of the famous children's book *The Hobbit* (1938), and the later trilogy, *The Lord of the Rings*, which has the same hobbit hero, Mr Bilbo Baggins, but is enjoyed more by older children and adults.

TOLSTOY, Count Alexei Konstantinovich (1817–75). Russian writer and poet. His lively interest in the popular sixteenth-century Russian epic brought him in contact with the peasant story-tellers who knew and recited folk poems which had been passed on by word of mouth and from one illiterate generation to another, but which survived nowhere else.

TOLSTOY, Count Lev Nikolayevich (1828–1910). Russian novelist, dramatist and thinker. He created an experimental pro-gressive school for the peasant children on his vast estate of Yasanya Polyana and some of his works were conceived for use in such schools: *Utro pomeschchika* (1852–6) (*A Landowner's Morning*), *Mnogo li cheloveky zemli nuzhno* (1886) (*Does a Man Need Much Earth?*).

TÖPFFER, Rudolph (1799–1846). Swiss-French illustrator, writer and educationalist, author of *Monsieur Vieuxbois* (1827), *Le Dr Festus* (1829), *Monsieur Cryptogamme* (1830), *Monsieur Persil* (1831), *Monsieur Crépin* (1837) which may be seen as the first comic strips.

TOWNSEND, J. R. Contemporary English writer of child-ren's books, author of *Gumble's Yard* (1961) a convincing portrayal of working-class neighbourhoods.

TRAVERS, Pamela. Contemporary English children's writer, author of *Mary Poppins* (1934), and its sequels.

TRIMMER, Sarah (1741–1810). English educationalist and editor of the edifying publication *The Family Magazine* (1778–89).

TWAIN, Mark (Samuel L. Clemens) (1835–1910). American writer, author of the famous children's books *Huckleberry Finn* (1884) and *The Adventures of Tom Sawyer* (1876).

UNGERER, Tomi. A contemporary French writer and illustrator living in Canada. He has revitalized the picture book and raised it to new heights. *The Three Robbers*, *Crictor* and *Zerelda's Ogre* are among his best-known books.

VAMBA (Luigi Bertelli) (1858–1920). Italian journalist and writer who edited a children's magazine, *Il giornalino della Domenica* (The Sunday Magazine), and himself wrote *Ciondolino* and *Il Giornalino di Gian Burrasca* (1905) (Gian Burrasca's Little Journal) which is as famous in Italy as *Pinocchio*. Although it does not have the poetic qualities of the latter, it does not suffer from heavy moralizing either.

VERNE, Jules (1828–1905). French adventure-story writer. He was of bourgeois stock and his childhood was uneventful, apart from an abortive attempt to stow away on an ocean liner. Later he went to try his luck in Paris as actor, journalist and scientist in turn, and only discovered his real vocation thanks to Hetzel who, on seeing an early draft of *Cinq semaines en Ballon*, undertook to publish the finished work (1863). All his books were published by Hetzel in *Le Magasin d'éducation et de récréation* and were conceived with the idea of introducing schoolboys to 'the saga of science'. Among his best-known works are *20,000 Leagues Beneath the Sea*, *Around the World in Eighty Days*, and *Journey to the Centre of the Earth*.

VILDRAC, Charles. Contemporary French writer born in 1882, author of *L'Ile rose* (1924), *La Colonie* (1930) and *Milo* (1933), which are children's books.

VIVIER, Colette. Contemporary French writer of children's books, author of *La Maison des petits bonheurs* which was awarded the Prix Jeunesse for 1939. In *L'Étoile polaire* (1953), *La Porte ouverte* (1955) and *Le Petit Théâtre* (1968) she has been most successful in creating a true image of working-class circles.

VORONKOVA, Liouba. Contemporary Soviet children's writer, author of *The Little Town Girl*.

WESTERMAN, Percy F. (1876–1960). British author of boy's adventure stories. He wrote his first one, *A Lad of Grit*, in 1908 and over the next fifty years wrote about 150 books with titles such as *Under the White Ensign*, *Winning his Wings* and *The Bulldog Breed*.

WIGGIN, Kate (1856–1923). American writer of children's books, author of *Rebecca of Sunnybrook Farm* (1902).

WILDE, Oscar (1854–1900). Dramatist, essayist, poet and wit who also found time to publish a delightful volume of fairy stories, *The Happy Prince* (1888).

WILDER, Laura Ingalls (1867–1957). American author of eight autobiographical novels depicting the life of a pioneer family, the first of which is *Little House in the Big Woods* (1932).

WINKLER-VONK. Annie. Contemporary Dutch writer of books for children, author of *Janny* (1952).

WINTERFELD, H. Contemporary German writer of books for children, author of *Timpetill* (1955).

WOLFEL, Ursula. Contemporary German writer of books for children, author of *Feuerschuh und Windsandale* (*Fire Shoes and Wind Sandals*).

WYSS, Johann Rudolf (1781–1830). Swiss writer and professor of philosophy at Bern, author of *The Swiss Family Robinson* (1812) the story of a family wrecked on a desert island.

YONGE, Charlotte M. (1823–1901). English writer whose popularity is nowadays difficult to understand unless one places her in her period – a time when the Oxford Movement was at its height. Her many works all portray the virtuous family life and the best known are *The Heir of Redclyffe* (1853), *The Little Duke* (1854), *The Daisy Chain* (1856) and *The Pillars of the House* (1873). From 1851 to 1890 she edited a magazine for girls called *The Monthly Packet*.

Index